Chapter and Unit Tests for English Language Learners and Special-Needs Students

with Answer Key

HOLT CALL TO FREEDOM

Beginnings to 1877

HOLT, RINEHART AND WINSTON

A Harcourt Education Company

Austin • New York • Orlando • Atlanta • San Francisco • Boston • Dallas • Toronto • London

Cover: Christie's Images

Printed in the United States of America

ISBN 0-03-065228-6

1 2 3 4 5 6 7 8 9 085 04 03 02 01

CHAPTER AND UNIT TESTS FOR ENGLISH LANGUAGE LEARNERS AND SPECIAL-NEEDS STUDENTS

UNIT 9 ★ A Growing America

★ TO THE TEACHER ★

Chapter and Unit Tests for English Language Learners and Special-Needs Students

with Answer Key

Each chapter and unit of *Call to Freedom: Beginnings to 1877* has a corresponding test designed to meet the needs of students who are continuing to acquire the English language. These tests use straightforward language and visuals, such as images and graphic organizers, to assess mastery of significant events, concepts, and issues in American history.

These tests can also be used for students who are having difficulty with the material. The tests are labeled *Form C* to distinguish them from the Chapter and Unit Tests, which are labeled *Form A* and *Form B*. All three types of tests require students to understand important aspects of the content, but provide a variety of assessment methods depending on students' needs.

CHAPTER 1

Name ______________________ Class ______________ Date ______________

The World before the Opening of the Atlantic FORM C

CHAPTER TEST

MATCHING *3 points each* Place the letters of the descriptions next to the appropriate terms.

_____ **1.** Mesoamerica

_____ **2.** archaeology

_____ **3.** artifacts

_____ **4.** vassals

_____ **5.** glyphs

_____ **6.** pueblos

_____ **7.** maize

_____ **8.** Anasazi

_____ **9.** Islam

_____ **10.** Berbers

a. symbols that represent ideas in early writing systems

b. built pueblos on mesas and cliffsides for defense

c. villages with buildings constructed of cut stone or adobe

d. traders in West Africa who used camels to carry goods across the desert

e. area including present-day Mexico and parts of Central America

f. study of the unwritten past

g. tools, weapons, and other objects made by humans

h. gave service to nobles during the Middle Ages in return for land

i. corn, a crop grown in North America and Mesoamerica

j. religion founded by Mohammad

FILL IN THE BLANK *2 points each* Choose from the following list to complete each of the statements below.

Jerusalem	Muslims	Aztec
Mississippian	migration	monasteries
totems	Kublai Khan	Magna Carta
matrilineal	Mali	Silk Road

1. The movement of people from one region to another is called ____________________ .

2. The people of the ____________________ culture built pyramid mounds out of solid earth in the area which is now Illinois.

3. The ____________________ created a large empire by conquering most of the groups living in central Mexico.

4. Native Americans in the Northwest carved tall poles with images of animal and ancestor spirits called ____________________ .

5. During the Crusades, Christians and Muslims fought for control of ____________________ .

6. During the Middle Ages, religious communities called ____________________ were the centers for learning and book production.

7. Cultures that trace their ancestry through their mothers rather than through their fathers are called ____________________ .

8. Timbuktu in the African kingdom of ____________________ became a center of Islamic culture and learning.

9. People who follow the teachings of Muhammad are called ____________________ .

10. In 1215 King John of England signed ____________________ , which said that even kings and queens had to obey the law.

11. The trading route stretching from the Black Sea into China was known as the ____________________ .

12. China began to trade with Arabia and India during the rule of ____________________ .

TRUE/FALSE *2 points each* Mark each statement *T* if it is true or *F* if it is false.

_____ 1. Domestication of plants and animals made it possible for some early people to settle in one place for long periods of time.

_____ 2. The Plains Indians depended on the mammoth for food, clothing, and shelter.

_____ 3. Native Americans of the Northwest Coast lived in a harsh desert environment.

_____ 4. Zhu Di led the Mongols in an invasion of China.

_____ 5. The Ming dynasty had a large fleet of trading ships that carried silk and porcelain to Arabia, Africa, and India.

_____ 6. Under the feudal system, vassals, serfs, and peasants worked for nobles.

_____ 7. Tikal was the capital of the Aztec Empire.

_____ 8. As a result of trade across continents, cultures exchanged knowledge and religious beliefs as well as goods.

IDENTIFICATION *3 points each* Complete the graphic organizer by selecting the name of a person or group from the following list and matching it to the correct achievements.

Pope Urban II
Aztec
Vikings
Maya
William of Normandy
Paleo-Indians
Mansa Musa
Zheng He
Leif Eriksson
Iroquois

NAME	ACHIEVEMENTS
	used conquest to establish an empire and maintain a trade network from the city of Tenochtitlán
	led voyage to North America and established the colony of Vinland
	created a political group made of five Northeastern tribes
	developed a unique ship with both ends curving upward
	crossed land bridge to become first Americans
	invaded England and set up records known as Domesday Book
	created calendars and mathematical and astronomical systems
	called for Christians to go on the Crusades
	impressed many with his wealth during pilgrimage to Mecca
	commanded a treasure fleet, bringing wealth and knowledge of other cultures to China

CHAPTER 2

Name ______________________ Class ____________ Date ____________

The Age of Exploration FORM C

CHAPTER TEST

MATCHING *3 points each* Place the letters of the descriptions next to the appropriate names.

_____ **1.** Henry Hudson

_____ **2.** Christopher Columbus

_____ **3.** Samuel de Champlain

_____ **4.** Vasco da Gama

_____ **5.** John Cabot

_____ **6.** Vasco Núñez de Balboa

_____ **7.** Jacques Cartier

_____ **8.** Johannes Gutenberg

_____ **9.** Juan Sebastián de Elcano

a. crossed Panama to see the "South Sea"

b. explored the St. Lawrence River

c. first European to sail around Cape of Good Hope and reach India

d. convinced Spanish rulers to support search for a route to Asia across the Atlantic

e. voyages were the basis of England's claim to land in North America

f. invented movable type for printing presses

g. traveled with Huron guides to Great Lakes

h. set adrift during mutiny

i. completed voyage around the world after the death of the original captain

FILL IN THE BLANK *2 points each* Choose from the following list to complete each of the statements below.

Northwest Passage	joint-stock company	convert
viceroy	caravel	*Reconquista*
Line of Demarcation	Renaissance	capital
Black Death	Treaty of Tordesillas	circumnavigate

1. The ____________________ divided Spain's territories from Portugal's.

2. The rebirth of interest in Greek and Roman art and learning was the ____________________.

3. Queen Isabella wanted Christopher Columbus to ____________________ the Taino to Christianity.

4. Ferdinand Magellan organized the first successful journey to ____________________ the globe.

5. Columbus asked to be made ____________________, or royal governor, of any lands he found.

6. About one third of the people in Europe died as a result of the ____________________ .

7. The ____________________ moved the boundary between Spanish and Portuguese territory to give Portugal more right to explore.

8. Money or property used to earn more money is called ____________________ .

9. A ____________________ was a small, fast ship.

10. At the end of the ____________________ the Moors were forced out of Spain.

11. A ____________________ gave people the chance to invest their money with less individual risk.

12. Many explorers wanted to find a route through or around North America called the ____________________ .

TRUE/FALSE *2 points each* Mark each statement *T* if it is true or *F* if it is false.

_____ **1.** During the Commercial Revolution the European economy grew weak.

_____ **2.** America was named for Amerigo Vespucci.

_____ **3.** Ferdinand Magellan did not complete his voyage because he died of bubonic plague.

_____ **4.** When Christopher Columbus landed on San Salvador, he knew he had reached a new continent.

_____ **5.** The astrolabe allowed navigators to chart their postion by the stars.

_____ **6.** Many European nations wanted to find a sea route to Asia because Venice had a monopoly on the Asian products that reached the Mediterranean.

_____ **7.** Bartolomeu Dias was the first European to sail around the tip of South America.

_____ **8.** Pedro Álvares Cabral discovered Brazil accidentally when his ship was blown off course.

_____ **9.** Portuguese explorers refused to trade for slaves.

_____ **10.** While preparing to explore the Pacific Ocean, Vasco Núñez de Balboa was executed for overthrowing the governor of Panama.

_____ **11.** Spain and Portugal had little conflict over exploration rights in North and South America.

IDENTIFICATION *3 points each* To understand the effects of the Columbian Exchange, select a plant, animal, or disease from the following list and write it in the correct space on the map below.

corn	potatoes	tobacco
cocoa	horses	cattle
smallpox	measles	typhus

Columbian Exchange

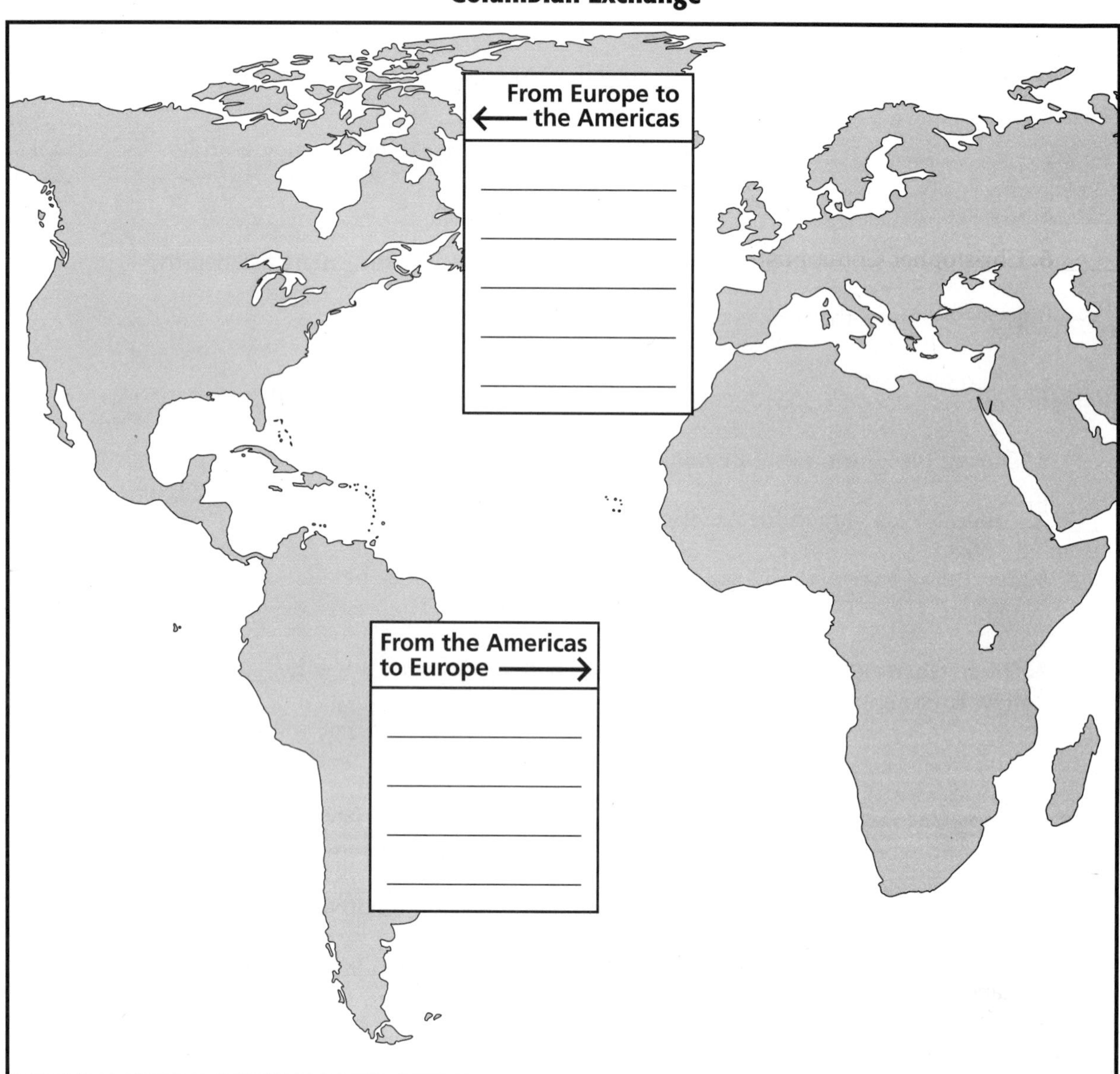

UNIT 1

Name ______________________ Class ______________ Date ______________

American Beginnings

FORM C

UNIT TEST

MATCHING *3 points each* Place the letters of the descriptions next to the appropriate names or terms.

_____ **1.** Henry Hudson

_____ **2.** vassals

_____ **3.** Vasco da Gama

_____ **4.** Johannes Gutenberg

_____ **5.** glyphs

_____ **6.** Christopher Columbus

_____ **7.** maize

_____ **8.** Samuel de Champlain

_____ **9.** Islam

_____ **10.** Vasco Núñez de Balboa

_____ **11.** Mesoamerica

a. symbols and pictures that represent ideas in early writing systems

b. traveled with Huron guides to the Great Lakes

c. corn grown in North America and Mesoamerica

d. first European to sail around Cape of Good Hope to India

e. Muslim religion founded by Mohammad

f. invented movable type for printing presses

g. crossed Panama to see the "South Sea"

h. gave service to nobles during the Middle Ages in return for land

i. area including present-day Mexico and parts of Central America

j. convinced king and queen of Spain to support search for a route to Asia across the Atlantic

k. set adrift during mutiny

FILL IN THE BLANK *2 points each* Choose from the following list to complete each of the statements below.

Jerusalem	*Reconquista*	Aztec
Mississippian	circumnavigate	monasteries
Renaissance	Muslims	Northwest Passage
Black Death	Silk Road	Magna Carta

1. The rebirth of interest in Greek and Roman art and learning was the ____________________ .

2. The people of the ____________________ culture built pyramid mounds out of solid earth in the area which is now Illinois.

3. The ____________________ created a large empire by conquering most of the groups living in central Mexico.

4. Ferdinand Magellan organized the first successful journey to ______________________ the globe.

5. During the Crusades, Christians and Muslims fought for control of ______________________ .

6. During the Middle Ages, religious communities called ______________________ were the centers for learning and book production.

7. Nearly one third of the people in Europe died as a result of the ______________________ .

8. During the ______________________ the Moors were forced out of Spain.

9. People who follow the teachings of Muhammad are called ______________________ .

10. In 1215 King John of England signed ______________________ , which said that even kings and queens had to obey the law.

11. The trading route stretching from the Black Sea into China were known as the ______________________ .

12. Many explorers wanted to find a route through or around North America called the ______________________.

TRUE/FALSE *2 points each* Mark each statement *T* if it is true or *F* if it is false.

_____ **1.** Domestication of plants and animals made it possible for some early people to settle in one place for long periods of time.

_____ **2.** During the Commercial Revolution the European economy grew stronger.

_____ **3.** When Christopher Columbus landed on San Salvador, he knew he had reached a new continent.

_____ **4.** The Plains Indians depended on the mammoth for food, clothing, and shelter.

_____ **5.** Many European nations wanted to find a sea route to Asia because Venice had a monopoly on the Asian products that reached the Mediterranean.

_____ **6.** Portuguese explorers refused to trade for slaves.

_____ **7.** The Ming dynasty had a large fleet of trading ships that carried silk and porcelain to Arabia, Africa, and India.

_____ **8.** Spain and Portugal had little conflict over exploration rights in North and South America.

IDENTIFICATION *3 points each* To understand the effects of the Columbian Exchange, select a plant, animal, or disease from the following list and write it in the correct space on the map below.

corn	potatoes	tobacco
cocoa	horses	cattle
smallpox	measles	typhus

Columbian Exchange

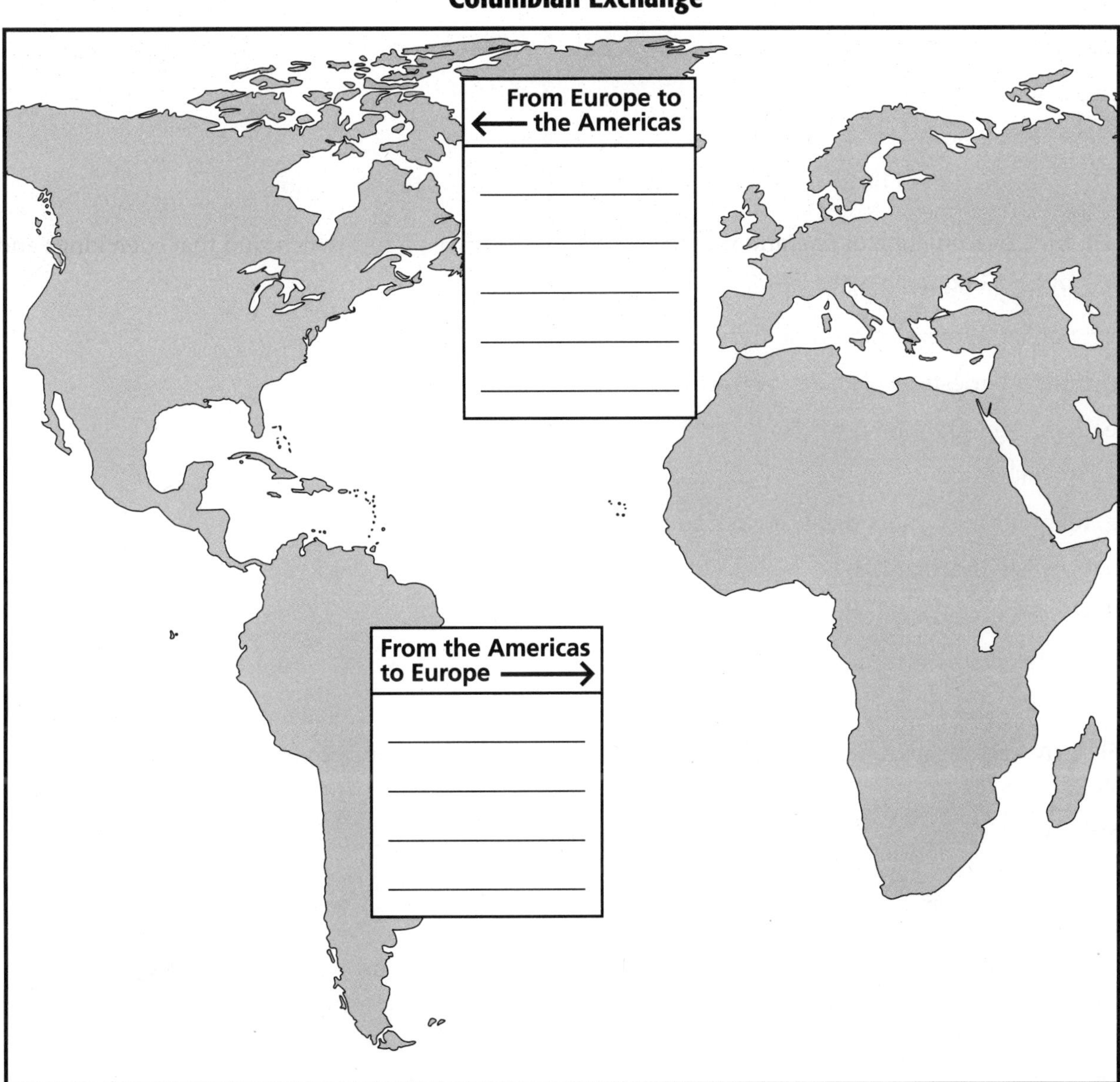

CHAPTER 3

Name ______________ Class ______________ Date ______________

New Empires in the Americas

FORM C

CHAPTER TEST

MATCHING *3 points each* Place the letters of the descriptions next to the appropriate terms.

_____ **1.** presidios

_____ **2.** Council of the Indies

_____ **3.** conquistadores

_____ **4.** missions

_____ **5.** El Camino Real

_____ **6.** Spanish Armada

_____ **7.** inflation

_____ **8.** charter

_____ **9.** pueblos

_____ **10.** Protestant Reformation

a. an increase in the amount of money in use and in the price of goods

b. formed to govern Spanish America

c. Spanish soldiers who led military expeditions to the Americas

d. built by priests as places to convert Indians to Christianity

e. document granting permission to start a colony

f. Spanish military forts

g. religious movement that tried to change the Catholic Church

h. Spanish fleet that fought English ships

i. served as trading posts

j. road that connected communities in New Spain

FILL IN THE BLANK *3 points each* Choose from the following list to complete each of the statements below.

New Amsterdam	plantation	England
Protestants	Aztec	Bartolomé de Las Casas
encomienda system	borderlands	New Netherland
Malintzin	sea dogs	Inca

1. The colony of ______________ was first settled by the Dutch West India Company.

2. The ______________ gave Spanish settlers the right to tax American Indians or demand labor from them in exchange for protecting them and teaching them skills and Christianity.

3. A large farm that specialized in growing one kind of crop was called a ______________.

4. Reformers known as ______________ hoped to change practices of the Catholic Church.

5. Few Europeans lived in the ______________, which began in northern Mexico and stretched northward.

6. Francisco Pizarro defeated the ____________________ Empire.

7. The ____________________ raided Spanish treasure ships.

8. Hernán Cortés defeated the ____________________ Empire.

9. King Philip II of Spain wanted to prevent ____________________ from helping Protestants in the Netherlands.

10. ____________________ helped Cortés, acting as an interpreter and adviser.

11. The settlement of ____________________ was built on Manhattan Island.

12. The priest named ____________________ wrote against mistreatment of American Indians in New Spain.

TRUE/FALSE *2 points each* Mark each statement *T* if it is true or *F* if it is false.

_____ **1.** Malintzin, also known as Malinche, was the leader of the Aztec Empire.

_____ **2.** All Spanish settlers thought slavery was evil.

_____ **3.** Many Protestants believed that the pope had too much power.

_____ **4.** The Spanish Armada successfully invaded England in 1588.

_____ **5.** Many Spanish explorers wanted to find gold and jewels.

_____ **6.** Spain's empire in the Americas was divided into the viceroyalty of Colombia and the viceroyalty of Mexico.

_____ **7.** French fur traders lived close to French settlements and tried to avoid American Indians.

_____ **8.** Some colonists were attracted to New Netherland because of the colony's policy of religious toleration.

_____ **9.** The Catholic Church was very important in Spanish settlement of the Americas.

IDENTIFICATION *2 points each* Complete the graphic organizer by selecting the name of a person or group from the following list and matching it to the correct achievements.

Juan Ponce de León
Álvar Núñez Cabeza de Vaca
René-Robert de La Salle
Francisco Vásquez de Coronado
Louis Jolliet and Jacques Marquette
Juan de Oñate
Hernando de Soto
Juan Rodríguez Cabrillo

NAME	ACTIONS
1. ______________________	established city of Santa Fe
2. ______________________	explored what is now New Mexico during search for Seven Cities of Cíbola
3. ______________________	searched Florida for Fountain of Youth
4. ______________________	followed Mississippi River to Gulf of Mexico
5. ______________________	traveled from what is now Texas to New Mexico after escaping from captivity among Indians
6. ______________________	traveled down Mississippi River as far as modern-day Arkansas
7. ______________________	explored coast of California
8. ______________________	became first European to cross the Mississippi River

CHAPTER 4

Name ______________________ Class ______________ Date ______________

The English Colonies — FORM C

CHAPTER TEST

MATCHING *2 points each* Place the letters of the descriptions next to the appropriate terms.

_____ **1.** John Smith	_____ **6.** Great Migration
_____ **2.** Nathaniel Bacon	_____ **7.** dissenters
_____ **3.** indentured servants	_____ **8.** town meetings
_____ **4.** Separatists	_____ **9.** proprietors
_____ **5.** headright	_____ **10.** Quakers

a. system in which colonists who paid their way to Virginia received 50 acres of land

b. religious sect that supported equality between sexes, religious tolerance, and nonviolence

c. people who disagree with official religious or political opinions

d. owners of a proprietary colony

e. took control of the Jamestown colony and forced the settlers to work and build better housing

f. those who wanted to cut all ties with the Church of England

g. people who signed contracts to work from four to seven years for those who paid their way to the American colonies

h. the movement of thousands of Puritans out of England

i. leader of a rebellion of former indentured servants against some friendly American Indians in order to take their land

j. gatherings in which each New England settlement discussed and decided local issues

FILL IN THE BLANK *3 points each* Choose from the following list to complete each of the statements below.

Toleration Act of 1649	New York	Massachusetts Bay Company
Powhatan Confederacy	Mayflower Compact	House of Burgesses
Thanksgiving	the Bible	Pennsylvania
joint-stock company	Salem witch trials	Catholics

1. When several investors agreed to share the cost and the risks of setting up a new colony, they formed a ______________________.

2. The ______________________ was a powerful alliance of Algonquian Indians.

3. Virginia's elected assembly was called the ______________________.

4. Puritan leaders argued that the most reliable source of authority within the church was ______________________ .

5. The legal contract that was one of the first attempts at self-government in the English colonies was called the ______________________ .

6. To celebrate their first harvest, the Plymouth colonists invited the Wampanoag Indians to share in the first ______________________ .

7. One group of Puritans got a charter to start a colony in New England; their group formed the ______________________ .

8. The ______________________ were fueled by a group of girls who accused people of casting spells on them.

9. Maryland was established so that ______________________ could practice their religion without fear of persecution.

10. One of the first efforts in the colonies to guarantee religious freedom for Christians was the ______________________ .

11. The Dutch colony of New Netherland became the English colony of ______________________ .

12. The colony of ______________________ grew rapidly because William Penn sold land at low prices and promised religious freedom for all Christians.

TRUE/FALSE *2 points each* Mark each statement *T* if it is true or *F* if it is false.

_____ **1.** The Jamestown colony had a rough start in part because the colonists searched for gold instead of planting crops and building homes.

_____ **2.** The Pilgrims landed near present-day Charleston.

_____ **3.** The Pilgrims were unhappy in the Netherlands because they were suffering under terrible religious persecution.

_____ **4.** The Massachusetts Bay Colony's charter gave it the right to govern itself as long as it followed the laws of England.

_____ **5.** Puritans thought that the three main duties of women were to obey their husbands, have children, and manage the household.

_____ **6.** Education was not of great importance in New England society.

_____ **7.** Maryland settlers apparently learned nothing from the experiences of the first Virginians since they repeated most of their mistakes.

_____ **8.** Colonists in the Dutch settlement of New Amsterdam were mostly fur traders and farmers.

_____ **9.** Director General Peter Stuyvesant took control of New Amsterdam and ruled it with kindness and fairness.

_____ **10.** James Oglethorpe, one of the founders of Georgia, hoped to establish a wealthy colony based on the plantation system and slavery.

ORGANIZING INFORMATION *3 points each* Draw a line from each colony listed on the left to each matching fact about that colony listed on the right.

	a. The second Lord Baltimore established this colony for Catholics.
1. Delaware	b. There were no towns or churches for a long time for this colony of poor farmers.
2. Georgia	c. People who paid their own way to this colony received land grants.
3. Maryland	d. This colony was once a Dutch colony called New Netherland.
4. New Jersey	e. This colony had a diverse population of Dutch, Swedes, Finns, and Scots.
5. New York	f. The founder of this colony was granted its charter because King Charles II owed the founder's father money.
6. North Carolina	g. This colony was once a part of Pennsylvania.
7. Pennsylvania	h. A founder of this colony outlawed slavery and limited land grants to 500 acres in hopes of keeping the colony from being controlled by large plantations.
8. South Carolina	

CHAPTER 5

Name ______________________ Class ______________ Date ______________

Life in the English Colonies

FORM C

CHAPTER TEST

MATCHING *3 points each* Place the letters of the descriptions next to the appropriate terms.

_____ **1.** Dominion of New England

_____ **2.** triangular trade

_____ **3.** Navigation Acts

_____ **4.** mercantilism

_____ **5.** libel

_____ **6.** duties

_____ **7.** slave codes

_____ **8.** revivals

_____ **9.** scientific method

_____ **10.** Enlightenment

a. trade network between the colonies, the West Indies, and Great Britain

b. false written statement that damages a person's reputation

c. laws passed to control slaves

d. government that united the New England colonies

e. movement in which thinkers used reason and logic to study human nature and society

f. taxes on goods brought into a country

g. careful examination of natural events and formation of theories from experiments and observations

h. practice of creating and keeping wealth by carefully controlling trade

i. laws that kept colonists from trading specified items with any country other than England

j. public church gatherings where masses of people came together to hear a minister's message

FILL IN THE BLANK *2 points each* Choose from the following list to complete each of the statements below.

trade	bicameral legislature	apprentices
Scientific Revolution	cash crops	Privy Council
imports	*New England Primer*	assemblies
Middle Passage	exports	staple crops

1. Colonists sometimes established ____________________ to make decisions and laws for them.

2. Officials wanted to create a favorable balance of ____________________ , in which more goods were sold to other countries than were bought from other countries.

3. Items purchased from other countries are ____________________ .

4. Africans were brought across the Atlantic in a brutal journey called the ____________________ .

5. Crops grown mainly to be sold for profits are called ____________________ .

6. The South's economy was based on agriculture and ____________________ , such as wood and tar.

7. Young boys called ____________________ learned skilled trades from master craftsmen.

8. The ____________________ was a group of royal advisers who set policy for England's colonies in North America.

9. The ____________________ was the movement in which scientists began re-examining the world and the universe.

10. The middle colonies produced ____________________ such as wheat and barley.

11. The ____________________ was a colonial teaching tool that had characters and stories from the Bible.

12. A ____________________ is a lawmaking body made up of two houses, or groups.

TRUE/FALSE *2 points each* Mark each statement *T* if it is true or *F* if it is false.

_____ **1.** The Privy Council generally allowed colonists to run their own affairs.

_____ **2.** The Great Awakening had little effect on colonial politics.

_____ **3.** The Quakers were the first group of colonists to make a public protest about the slave trade.

_____ **4.** Slave labor was not an important part of the New England economy because farm families used their own labor to plant and raise crops.

_____ **5.** The greatest part of the middle colonies' need for labor was filled by apprentices.

_____ **6.** Many women and African Americans became interested in the messages of the Great Awakening.

_____ **7.** Fishing and shipbuilding were not very important to the New England economy.

_____ **8.** During the 1700s architecture and home furnishings improved in style and quality.

IDENTIFICATION *3 points each* Complete the graphic organizer by selecting the name of a person from the following list and matching it to the correct description.

Galileo Galilei
Sir Isaac Newton
John Locke
David Rittenhouse
Benjamin Banneker
Benjamin Franklin
Jonathan Edwards
Anne Bradstreet
Phillis Wheatley
John Smibert

NAME	DESCRIPTION
1. ______________________	African American astronomer who accurately predicted an eclipse in 1789 and published an almanac
2. ______________________	New England poet who wrote about her love for her family and her religious faith
3. ______________________	European painter who came to paint and teach in America and who held the first art exhibit in the colonies
4. ______________________	second president of the American Philosophical Society who designed mathematical and astronomical instruments
5. ______________________	scientist who confirmed the theory that the planets revolve around the sun
6. ______________________	colonial inventor and scientist who identified positive and negative charges in electricity
7. ______________________	African American poet who wrote about the importance of Christianity in her life
8. ______________________	physicist who developed theories about motion and gravity
9. ______________________	Enlightenment philosopher who believed that people had natural rights to equality and liberty
10. ______________________	religious leader who helped develop the American style of dramatic sermons

UNIT 2

Name ______________________ Class ______________ Date ______________

Colonies in the Americas **FORM C**

★ ★ ★ ★ ★ ★ ★ ★ ★ ★ ★ ★ ★ ★ ★ ★ ★ ★ ★ ★

UNIT TEST

MATCHING *3 points each* Place the letters of the descriptions next to the appropriate terms.

_____ **1.** indentured servants

_____ **2.** Council of the Indies

_____ **3.** conquistadores

_____ **4.** Navigation Acts

_____ **5.** Great Migration

_____ **6.** Spanish Armada

_____ **7.** Enlightenment

_____ **8.** triangular trade

_____ **9.** Quakers

_____ **10.** Nathaniel Bacon

a. the movement of thousands of Puritans out of England

b. formed to govern Spanish America

c. Spanish soldiers who led military expeditions to the Americas

d. trade network between the colonies, the West Indies, and Great Britain

e. religious sect that believed in equality between the sexes, religious tolerance, and nonviolence

f. people who signed contracts to work from four to seven years for those who paid their way to the American colonies

g. led a rebellion against peaceful American Indians in order to take control of their land

h. Spanish fleet that fought English ships

i. movement in which thinkers used reason and logic to study human nature and society

j. laws that kept colonists from trading specified items with any country other than England

FILL IN THE BLANK *3 points each* Choose from the following list to complete each of the statements below.

Mayflower Compact	Catholics	*New England Primer*
Middle Passage	Aztec	bicameral legislature
encomienda system	New Amsterdam	Protestants
Powhatan Confederacy	sea dogs	House of Burgesses

1. Africans were brought across the Atlantic in a brutal journey called the ______________________.

2. The ______________________ gave Spanish settlers the right to tax Indians or demand labor from them in exchange for protecting them and teaching them skills and Christianity.

3. Virginia's elected assembly was called the ______________________.

4. Reformers known as ______________________ hoped to change practices of the Catholic Church.

5. The legal contract that established the Plymouth colony was called the ______________________.

6. The ______________________ was a colonial teaching tool that contained characters and stories from the Bible.

7. The ______________________ raided Spanish treasure ships.

8. Hernán Cortés defeated the ______________________ Empire.

9. The ______________________ was a powerful alliance of Algonquian Indians.

10. A ______________________ is a lawmaking body made up of two houses, or groups.

11. The colony of ______________________ was built on Manhattan Island.

12. Maryland was established so that ______________________ could practice their religion without fear of persecution.

TRUE/FALSE *2 points each* Mark each statement *T* if it is true or *F* if it is false.

_____ 1. The Jamestown colony had a rough start in part because the colonists searched for gold instead of planting crops and building homes.

_____ 2. James Oglethorpe, one of the founders of Georgia, hoped to establish a wealthy colony based on the plantation system and slavery.

_____ 3. Many Protestants believed that the pope had too much power.

_____ 4. The Quakers were the first group of colonists to make a public protest about the slave trade.

_____ 5. Many Spanish explorers wanted to find gold and jewels.

_____ 6. Education was not of great importance in New England society.

_____ 7. French fur traders lived close to French settlements and tried to avoid Indians.

_____ 8. The Great Awakening had little effect on colonial politics.

_____ 9. Fishing and shipbuilding were not very important to the New England economy.

IDENTIFICATION *2 points each* Complete the graphic organizer by selecting the name of a person or group from the following list and matching it to the correct achievements.

Juan Ponce de León
Álvar Núñez Cabeza de Vaca
René-Robert de La Salle
Francisco Vásquez de Coronado
Louis Jolliet and Jacques Marquette
Juan de Oñate
Hernando de Soto
Juan Rodríguez Cabrillo

NAME	ACTIONS
1. ______________________	established city of Santa Fe
2. ______________________	explored what is now New Mexico during search for Seven Cities of Cíbola
3. ______________________	searched Florida for Fountain of Youth
4. ______________________	followed Mississippi River to Gulf of Mexico
5. ______________________	traveled from what is now Texas to New Mexico after escaping from captivity among Indians
6. ______________________	traveled down Mississippi River as far as modern-day Arkansas
7. ______________________	explored coast of California
8. ______________________	became first European to cross the Mississippi River

CHAPTER 6

Name ______________________ Class ______________ Date ______________

Conflicts in the Colonies

FORM C

CHAPTER TEST

MATCHING *3 points each* Place the letters of the descriptions next to the appropriate terms.

______ **1.** writs of assistance

______ **2.** pioneers

______ **3.** militia

______ **4.** backcountry

______ **5.** casualties

______ **6.** propaganda

______ **7.** Proclamation of 1763

______ **8.** Sugar Act

______ **9.** Townshend Acts

______ **10.** Sons of Liberty

a. killed, injured, or captured soldiers

b. information giving only one side of an argument

c. area between settled areas on the coast and the Appalachian Mountains

d. special search warrants that allowed officials to search for smuggled items

e. banned any more settlement west of the Appalachian Mountains

f. set taxes on molasses and sugar brought into the colonies

g. secret groups that sometimes used violence to frighten tax collectors

h. people who first settle an area

i. civilians who serve as soldiers

j. put taxes on imported glass, lead, paints, paper, and tea

FILL IN THE BLANK *3 points each* Choose from the following list to complete each of the statements below.

Stamp Act	Boston Massacre	Albany Plan of Union
Metacomet	Edward Braddock	James Otis
James Wolfe	Pontiac's Rebellion	Fort Duquesne
Boston Tea Party	George Grenville	Committees of Correspondence

1. The first real battle of the French and Indian War took place at ______________________ .

2. Prime Minister ______________________ thought the colonists should be taxed to pay Britain's war debts.

3. Because ______________________ compared himself to King Charles II of England, the settlers called him King Philip.

4. The ______________________ called for colonists to join together under a president general and a grand council.

5. General ______________________ was ambushed while approaching Fort Duquesne.

6. The ______________________ wrote letters to other colonies to share information.

7. British troops fired into an angry crowd and killed five people during the ______________________ .

8. The ______________________ forced colonists to pay a special tax for anything printed on paper.

9. General ______________________ led a successful British attack on Quebec.

10. ______________________ argued that no one could be taxed without their consent.

11. During the ______________________ , colonists disguised as Indians dumped more than 340 chests of tea into Boston Harbor.

12. A number of Indian tribes attacked Fort Detroit and other British forts during ______________________ .

TRUE/FALSE *2 points each* Mark each statement *T* if it is true or *F* if it is false.

_____ 1. King William's War led to the deaths of some 600 colonists and about 3,000 Indians.

_____ 2. Samuel Adams thought that Parliament had the right to tax the colonists without their permission.

_____ 3. People in London and in the colonies wanted Parliament to repeal the Stamp Act.

_____ 4. The Townshend Acts gave more power to colonial courts.

_____ 5. Colonial merchants thought the Tea Act would cause them to lose money.

_____ 6. The Intolerable Acts were passed as punishment for the Boston Tea Party.

_____ 7. Mercy Otis Warren wrote plays and essays that supported the British government's actions.

_____ 8. In Virginia, Patrick Henry made a speech asking the House of Burgesses to oppose the Stamp Act.

_____ 9. Crispus Attucks was a British soldier accused of killing people during the Boston Massacre.

_____ 10. After the French and Indian War, Britain had a claim to all lands east of the Mississippi River.

IDENTIFICATION *7 points each* Examine the drawing below and answer the questions that follow.

1. What does this sign ask for?

____

____

2. Who might have put up this sign?

____

____

CHAPTER 7

Name ______________________ Class ______________ Date ______________

The American Revolution FORM C

CHAPTER TEST

MATCHING *3 points each* Place the letters of the descriptions next to the appropriate terms.

_____ **1.** Patriots

_____ **2.** mercenaries

_____ **3.** Redcoats

_____ **4.** Olive Branch Petition

_____ **5.** siege

_____ **6.** Loyalists

_____ **7.** Minutemen

_____ **8.** Lord Dunmore's Proclamation

_____ **9.** guerrilla warfare

_____ **10.** Battle of Saratoga

a. nickname for British soldiers

b. swift, hit-and-run attacks

c. nickname for members of the Massachusetts militia

d. military blockade of a city or fort

e. colonists who remained loyal to Great Britain

f. peace request sent by the Second Continental Congress

g. offered freedom to slaves who would fight for the British

h. colonists who fought for independence

i. hired foreign soldiers

j. Patriot victory that led to formal declaration of support from French

FILL IN THE BLANK *2 points each* Choose from the following list to complete each of the statements below.

Thomas Paine	Francis Marion	Comte de Rochambeau
Deborah Sampson	Friedrich von Steuben	George Washington
Thomas Jefferson	Marquis de Lafayette	William Howe
John Paul Jones	Thayendanegea	Salem Poor

1. Some women such as ____________________ wore men's clothing and fought in battles.

2. The Second Continental Congress chose ____________________ to lead the Continental Army.

3. *Common Sense* was a pamphlet written by ____________________ , who thought the colonies should break away from Great Britain.

4. Naval hero ____________________ captured the British warship *Serapis* even though his ship's heaviest artillery had been destroyed.

5. Although some African Americans such as ____________________ had fought in early battles, Washington initially prohibited them from joining the Continental Army.

6. The ____________________ came from France to join the Continental Army.

7. Patriots and Redcoats both referred to ____________________ as "The Swamp Fox" because the British could not capture him.

8. Baron ____________________ used his military experience in Prussia to teach basic drills to the Continental Army.

9. Much of the Declaration of Independence was written by ____________________ .

10. Mohawk leader ____________________ fought for the British.

11. The ____________________ brought a large French force to New York to support Washington's soldiers.

12. Under the command of General ____________________ , the British drove the Continental Army out of Long Island.

TRUE/FALSE *2 points each* Mark each statement *T* if it is true or *F* if it is false.

_____ **1.** Hessian troops defeated the Patriots at the Battle of Trenton.

_____ **2.** About one fourth of Washington's soldiers died at Valley Forge during the winter of 1777–78.

_____ **3.** The first battle of the American Revolution took place in Camden, South Carolina.

_____ **4.** George Rogers Clark led attacks on British forts on the western frontier.

_____ **5.** The Battle of Bunker Hill proved that the colonists could not defeat the British.

_____ **6.** As the governor of Spanish Louisiana, Bernardo de Gálvez supported the British.

_____ **7.** The Treaty of Paris of 1783 ended the war.

_____ **8.** Polish officer Casimir Pulaski organized and trained Patriot cavalry units.

_____ **9.** In 1781 the British surrendered after losing the Battle of Yorktown.

_____ **10.** The British won the Battle of Princeton because they took the Patriots by surprise.

_____ **11.** In 1775 Patriot forces captured British weapons at Fort Ticonderoga.

_____ **12.** The Declaration of Independence did not include women and African Americans.

_____ **13.** In 1776 Washington drove the British out of Boston.

_____ **14.** Benedict Arnold supported the Patriots throughout the war.

IDENTIFICATION *3 points each* Determine whether the actions listed below were taken by the First Continental Congress or the Second Continental Congress. Write the letter of each action in the appropriate box.

a. recommended that colonists continue to boycott British goods

b. made plans to organize and fund the Continental Army to defend the colonies

c. sent the Olive Branch Petition to King George III as a final attempt at peace

d. warned militias to be prepared

e. chose George Washington to command the army

f. sent the Declaration of Resolves to King George III, demanding the right of the colonists to "life, liberty, and property"

CONGRESS	First Continental Congress	Second Continental Congress
DATE ORGANIZED	September 1774	May 1775
MEETING LOCATION	Philadelphia	Philadelphia
ACTIONS TAKEN	1. ______________	2. ______________

UNIT 3

Name ______________________ Class ______________ Date ______________

The Colonies Break Free — FORM C

UNIT TEST

MATCHING *3 points each* Place the letters of the descriptions next to the appropriate terms.

_____ **1.** writs of assistance

_____ **2.** Patriots

_____ **3.** militia

_____ **4.** Lord Dunmore's Proclamation

_____ **5.** guerrilla warfare

_____ **6.** Redcoats

_____ **7.** Proclamation of 1763

_____ **8.** Loyalists

_____ **9.** Townshend Acts

_____ **10.** Sons of Liberty

a. nickname for British soldiers

b. special search warrants that allowed tax collectors to search for smuggled items

c. banned any more settlement west of the Appalachian Mountains

d. colonists who fought for independence

e. offered freedom to slaves who would fight for the British

f. colonists who remained loyal to Great Britain

g. secret groups that sometimes used violence to frighten tax collectors

h. swift, hit-and-run attacks

i. civilians who serve as soldiers

j. put taxes on imported glass, lead, paints, paper, and tea

FILL IN THE BLANK *3 points each* Choose from the following list to complete each of the statements below.

Stamp Act	Boston Massacre	Albany Plan of Union
Marquis de Lafayette	George Washington	Friedrich von Steuben
James Wolfe	Comte de Rochambeau	Thomas Paine
Boston Tea Party	George Grenville	Thomas Jefferson

1. *Common Sense* was a pamphlet written by ______________________, who thought the colonies should break away from Great Britain.

2. Colonists opposed the taxes suggested by Prime Minister ______________________, who wanted to pay Britain's war debts.

3. Baron ______________________ used his military experience in Prussia to teach basic drills to the Continental Army.

4. The ____________________ called for colonists to join together under a president general and a grand council.

5. Much of the Declaration of Independence was written by ____________________ .

6. The Second Continental Congress chose ____________________ to lead the Continental Army.

7. British troops fired into an angry crowd and killed five people during the ____________________ .

8. The ____________________ forced colonists to pay a special tax for anything printed on paper.

9. General ____________________ led a successful British attack on Quebec.

10. The ____________________ came from France to join the Continental Army.

11. During the ____________________, colonists disguised as Indians dumped more than 340 chests of tea into Boston Harbor.

12. The ____________________ brought a large French force to New York to support Washington's soldiers.

TRUE/FALSE *2 points each* Mark each statement *T* if it is true or *F* if it is false.

_____ 1. As the governor of Spanish Louisiana, Bernardo de Gálvez supported the British.

_____ 2. Samuel Adams thought that Parliament had the right to tax the colonists without their permission.

_____ 3. In 1781 the British surrendered after losing the Battle of Yorktown.

_____ 4. The Townshend Acts gave more power to colonial courts.

_____ 5. Colonial merchants thought the Tea Act would cause them to lose money.

_____ 6. The Intolerable Acts were passed as punishment for the Boston Tea Party.

_____ 7. The Declaration of Independence did not include women and African Americans.

_____ 8. In Virginia, Patrick Henry made a speech asking the House of Burgesses to oppose the Stamp Act.

_____ 9. The Treaty of Paris of 1783 ended the war.

_____ 10. George Rogers Clark led attacks on British forts along the Atlantic coast.

_____ 11. The first battle of the American Revolution took place in Camden, South Carolina.

IDENTIFICATION *2 points each* Determine whether the actions listed below were taken by the First Continental Congress or the Second Continental Congress. Write the number of each action in the appropriate box.

1. recommended that colonists continue to boycott British goods

2. made plans to organize and fund the Continental Army to defend the colonies

3. sent the Olive Branch Petition to King George III as a final attempt at peace

4. warned militias to be prepared

5. chose George Washington to command the army

6. sent the Declaration of Resolves to King George III, demanding the right of the colonists to "life, liberty, and property"

CONGRESS	First Continental Congress	Second Continental Congress
DATE ORGANIZED	September 1774	May 1775
MEETING LOCATION	Philadelphia	Philadelphia
ACTIONS TAKEN	____________________	____________________

CHAPTER 8

Name ______________________ Class ______________ Date ______________

Forming a Government

FORM C

CHAPTER TEST

MATCHING *3 points each* Place the letters of the descriptions next to the appropriate terms.

_____ **1.** tariffs

_____ **2.** republic

_____ **3.** creditors

_____ **4.** amendments

_____ **5.** New Jersey Plan

_____ **6.** popular sovereignty

_____ **7.** debtors

_____ **8.** constitution

_____ **9.** Virginia Plan

a. people who borrow money

b. suggested that representatives be chosen on the basis of state population

c. idea that political authority rests with the people

d. taxes on imports or exports

e. set of principles and laws that state the powers and duties of the government

f. people who lend money

g. government in which the people hold power and elect representatives

h. suggested that every state have the same number of representatives

i. official changes, corrections, or additions

FILL IN THE BLANK *2 points each* Choose from the following list to complete each of the statements below.

bill of rights	Federalists	Northwest Territory
depression	Constitutional Convention	checks and balances
Federalist Papers	federalism	interstate commerce
suffrage	Three-Fifths Compromise	Antifederalists

1. Trade between two or more states is called ______________________ .

2. Many state constitutions expanded ______________________ , or voting rights.

3. Twelve of the 13 states sent delegates to the ______________________ in Philadelphia to discuss changes to the Articles of Confederation.

4. James Madison, Alexander Hamilton, and John Jay wrote the ______________________ to convince people to support the Constitution.

5. The ______________________ was an attempt to end conflict over how to determine the population of southern states for purposes of representation.

6. People who wanted a stronger central government were known as ____________________ .

7. The decision to pay war debts by taxing land led to an economic ____________________ in Massachusetts.

8. The Northwest Ordinance of 1787 created the ____________________ and provided a way for new states to join the nation.

9. The distribution of power between a central government and state governments is called ____________________ .

10. A number of states refused to ratify the Constitution unless they were promised that a ____________________ would be added.

11. People who wanted most power to be in the hands of the states were called ____________________ .

12. The Constitution is based on a system of ____________________ to keep any one part of the government from becoming too strong.

TRUE/FALSE *2 points each* Mark each statement *T* if it is true or *F* if it is false.

_____ **1.** John Adams and Thomas Jefferson played important roles in writing the Constitution.

_____ **2.** The Great Compromise gave each state two votes in the upper house of the legislature as well as votes based on population in the lower house.

_____ **3.** The Constitution allowed the slave trade to continue for another 20 years.

_____ **4.** The first state to ratify the Constitution was Massachusetts.

_____ **5.** The Land Ordinance of 1785 included Thomas Jefferson's ideas about religious freedom.

_____ **6.** The Articles of Confederation provided a weak central government that encountered many problems in the early years of the republic.

_____ **7.** Most American leaders thought that Enlightenment ideas were out-of-date.

_____ **8.** Massachusetts farmers joined Shays's Rebellion to protest the Constitution.

_____ **9.** Spanish officials closed the lower Mississippi to U.S. shipping in 1784, angering many western farmers.

_____ **10.** The Mayflower Compact was the first written constitution in the English colonies.

_____ **11.** Antifederalists such as Patrick Henry feared that a strong central government would be uncontrollable.

IDENTIFICATION *3 points each* Complete the following chart to show the makeup and the responsibilities of the three branches of the federal government. Write the letter of each listed item in the appropriate box.

a. proposing bills

b. interpreting laws

c. punishing criminals

d. passing laws

e. president and administrative departments

f. enforcing laws

g. Senate and House of Representatives

h. national courts

i. settling disputes between states

BRANCH	MADE UP OF	RESPONSIBLE FOR
Legislative	1. __________	2. __________
Executive	3. __________	4. __________
Judicial	5. __________	6. __________

Name ______________ Class ____________ Date ____________

CHAPTER 9

Citizenship and the Constitution — FORM C

CHAPTER TEST

MATCHING *3 points each* Place the letters of the descriptions next to the appropriate terms.

_____ **1.** subpoena

_____ **2.** naturalization

_____ **3.** veto

_____ **4.** elastic clause

_____ **5.** executive order

_____ **6.** impeach

_____ **7.** delegated powers

_____ **8.** double jeopardy

_____ **9.** bail

_____ **10.** eminent domain

a. to cancel legislation

b. being tried again for the same crime in the same jurisdiction

c. money paid to allow a person to stay out of jail until trial

d. order to appear in court

e. power of the government to take private property for public use

f. process of gaining citizenship

g. bring charges against the president

h. allows Congress to increase its power to address new issues

i. granted to the federal government only

j. command issued by the president, that has the effect of law

FILL IN THE BLANK *3 points each* Choose from the following list to complete each of the statements below.

representative democracy	jury	First
political action committees	cabinet	due process
apportionment	six	deport
pardons	citizen	search warrant

1. Congress examines changes in state populations to determine the ______________________, or distribution, of representatives.

2. To conduct a search of a person's property, authorities usually must first obtain a ______________________, which is a judge's order authorizing the search.

3. If an immigrant breaks the law, the government has the right to ______________________ that person.

4. A ______________________ is a government by representatives of the people.

5. According to the Fifth Amendment, no one may be punished for a crime without ____________________ , or the fair application, of the law.

6. Organizations called ____________________ collect money to distribute to candidates who support the same issues as the contributors.

7. The term for a senator is ____________________ years.

8. The heads of the 14 executive departments make up the ____________________ .

9. Freedom of religion is a basic right guaranteed in the ____________________ Amendment.

10. All U.S. citizens can be called for ____________________ duty, which involves listening to a court case and reaching a verdict on it.

11. People born in a foreign country can become U.S. citizens if one of their parents is a ____________________ .

12. The president has the power to grant ____________________ , or freedom from punishment, for a person convicted of a federal crime or who is facing criminal charges.

TRUE/FALSE *2 points each* Mark each statement *T* if it is true or *F* if it is false.

_____ **1.** The number of justices on the Supreme Court varies from year to year.

_____ **2.** The House of Representatives and the Senate make up the legislative branch of the U.S. government.

_____ **3.** Only the president has the power to declare war through an executive order.

_____ **4.** Antifederalists believed in a strong central government.

_____ **5.** Both federal and state governments can levy taxes.

_____ **6.** The First Amendment of the Constitution includes freedom from hunger.

_____ **7.** People accused of crimes have a right to legal services even if they cannot pay for them.

_____ **8.** Even though the United States now has a volunteer army, young men must still register for the draft at age 18.

IDENTIFICATION *3 points each* Complete the graphic organizer by writing the powers listed below in the correct column to show which branch of government has that power.

- regulating education
- taxing
- declaring war
- enforcing laws
- conducting elections
- running the postal system

POWERS DELEGATED TO THE FEDERAL GOVERNMENT	POWERS RETAINED BY THE STATE GOVERNMENT OR BY CITIZENS	POWERS SHARED BY FEDERAL AND STATE GOVERNMENTS
coining money	regulating trade within states	borrowing money
regulating interstate and international trade	establishing local governments	providing for citizens' welfare
conducting diplomacy	3. ____________	5. ____________
providing for national defense	4. ____________	6. ____________
1. ____________		
2. ____________		

CHAPTER 10

Name ______________________ Class ______________ Date ______________

Launching the Nation

FORM C

CHAPTER TEST

MATCHING *3 points each* Place the letters of the descriptions next to the appropriate terms.

_____ **1.** privateers

_____ **2.** Jay's Treaty

_____ **3.** national debt

_____ **4.** Treaty of Greenville

_____ **5.** Alien and Sedition Acts

_____ **6.** John Jay

_____ **7.** Pinckney's Treaty

_____ **8.** loose construction

_____ **9.** protective tariff

_____ **10.** Neutrality Proclamation

a. agreement in which the British promised to abandon their forts on the western frontier

b. agreement that gave the United States access to some Indian lands in the Northwest Territory

c. the amount of money owed by the United States

d. private ships authorized to attack a country's enemies

e. made it illegal for U.S. citizens to plot together to oppose the federal government

f. first Chief Justice of the United States

g. a duty, or tax, on goods brought into the country that raises the price of those goods

h. belief that the federal government can do anything reasonable unless specifically prohibited by the Constitution

i. agreement in which Spain changed the Florida border and reopened the port of New Orleans

j. proclamation that stated that the United States would remain neutral toward all nations at war in Europe

FILL IN THE BLANK *3 points each* Choose from the following list to complete each of the statements below.

speculators
Bank of the United States
precedent
Twelfth Amendment
Edmond Genet
Farewell Address
Whiskey Rebellion
XYZ affair
Judiciary Act
U.S. Army
bonds
political parties

1. The ____________________ created a separate ballot for president and vice president.

2. Congress established a federal court system when it passed the ____________________ in 1789.

3. French minister ____________________ traveled through the United States to gather support for the French Revolution.

4. In his ____________________, President Washington warned Americans to avoid public debt, dangerous foreign alliances, and political divisions at home.

5. Groups that organize to help elect government officials and to influence government policies are called ______________________ .

6. Certificates that represent money owed by the government to private citizens are called ______________________ .

7. A ______________________ is an action or decision that later serves as an example.

8. The ______________________ defeated a confederation of American Indians in the Battle of Fallen Timbers.

9. In the ______________________, French agents told U.S. diplomats that France would discuss a treaty only in exchange for a bribe and a loan from the U.S. government.

10. Farmers in regions such as western Pennsylvania tarred and feathered tax collectors during the ______________________ .

11. Investors called ______________________ buy items at low prices in the hope that the value will increase later.

12. Alexander Hamilton planned the ______________________ to improve the U.S. economy.

TRUE/FALSE *2 points each* Mark each statement *T* if it is true or *F* if it is false.

______ **1.** Most Americans lived in cities in the late 1700s.

______ **2.** Alexander Hamilton believed that the best way to expand the U.S. economy was through manufacturing.

______ **3.** The U.S. government supported the French Revolution.

______ **4.** The Battle of Fallen Timbers led to an agreement that U.S. settlers could not travel through Indian lands.

______ **5.** John Adams won the 1796 election as a member of the Federalist Party.

______ **6.** Strict construction of the Constitution is the idea that the government could take reasonable actions that the Constitution did not specifically forbid it from taking.

______ **7.** In 1793 Jefferson resigned his position as secretary of state because he was upset by the U.S. policy toward France and because he felt Hamilton was influencing the president's opinion too much.

______ **8.** The French Revolution restored the monarchy to France.

IDENTIFICATION *3 points each* Use the information listed below to complete the following graphic organizer about the positions of Alexander Hamilton and Thomas Jefferson on important issues.

- loose construction
- federal government should pay full price
- paying full price cheats original owners
- should not create a national bank
- majority should rule
- should come from manufacturing

ISSUE	HAMILTON	JEFFERSON
Buying back bonds	1. ______	2. ______
Faith in common people	little	3. ______
Promoting economic growth	4. ______	should come from agriculture
Creating a national bank	should create a national bank	5. ______
Interpreting the Constitution	6. ______	strict construction

UNIT 4

Name ______________________ Class ______________ Date ______________

A New American Nation

FORM C

UNIT TEST

MATCHING *3 points each* Place the letters of the descriptions next to the appropriate terms.

_____ **1.** delegated power

_____ **2.** Pinckney's Treaty

_____ **3.** elastic clause

_____ **4.** amendments

_____ **5.** New Jersey Plan

_____ **6.** Jay's Treaty

_____ **7.** double jeopardy

_____ **8.** Neutrality Proclamation

_____ **9.** Virginia Plan

_____ **10.** impeach

a. being tried again for the same crime in the same jurisdiction

b. suggested that representatives be chosen on the basis of state population

c. agreement that reopened the port of New Orleans to U.S. shipping

d. statement that the United States would remain neutral toward all nations at war in Europe

e. agreement in which the British promised to abandon their forts on the western frontier

f. granted to the federal government only

g. allows Congress to increase its power to cover new issues

h. bring charges against the president

i. official changes, corrections, or additions

j. suggested that every state have the same number of representatives

FILL IN THE BLANK *2 points each* Choose from the following list to complete each of the statements below.

bill of rights	apportionment	Whiskey Rebellion
search warrant	Constitutional Convention	representative democracy
Federalist Papers	XYZ affair	Edmond Genet
Bank of the United States	Three-Fifths Compromise	cabinet

1. To conduct a search of a person's property, authorities usually must first obtain a ______________________, which is a judge's order authorizing the search.

2. French minister ______________________ traveled through the United States to gather support for the French Revolution.

3. Twelve of the 13 states sent delegates to the ______________________ in Philadelphia to discuss changes to the Articles of Confederation.

4. James Madison, Alexander Hamilton, and John Jay wrote the ____________________ to convince people to support the Constitution.

5. The ____________________ was an attempt to end conflict over how to determine the population of southern states for purposes of representation.

6. A ____________________ is a government by representatives of the people.

7. Alexander Hamilton planned the ____________________ to improve the U.S. economy.

8. The heads of the 14 executive departments make up the ____________________.

9. Farmers in regions such as western Pennsylvania tarred and feathered tax collectors during the ____________________.

10. A number of states refused to ratify the Constitution unless they were promised that a ____________________ would be added.

11. In the ____________________, French agents told U.S. diplomats that France would discuss a treaty only in exchange for a bribe and a loan from the U.S. government.

12. Congress examines changes in state populations to determine the ____________________, or distribution, of representatives.

TRUE/FALSE *2 points each* Mark each statement *T* if it is true or *F* if it is false.

_____ **1.** The House of Representatives and the Senate make up the legislative branch of the U.S. government.

_____ **2.** The Great Compromise gave each state two votes in the upper house of the legislature as well as votes based on population in the lower house.

_____ **3.** The Constitution allowed the slave trade to continue for another 20 years.

_____ **4.** The French Revolution restored the monarchy to France.

_____ **5.** The Articles of Confederation provided a weak central government that encountered many problems in the early years of the republic.

_____ **6.** Strict construction is the idea that the federal government could take reasonable actions that the Constitution did not specifically forbid it from taking.

_____ **7.** Massachusetts farmers joined Shays's Rebellion to protest the Constitution.

_____ **8.** Antifederalists believed in a strong central government.

_____ **9.** The Battle of Fallen Timbers led to an agreement that stated that U.S. settlers could travel through Indian lands.

_____**10.** The U.S. government supported the French Revolution.

_____**11.** People accused of crimes have a right to legal services even if they cannot pay for them.

IDENTIFICATION *4 points each* Use the information listed below to complete the following graphic organizer about the positions of Alexander Hamilton and Thomas Jefferson on important issues.

- loose construction
- federal government should pay full price
- paying full price cheats original owners
- should not create a national bank
- majority should rule
- should come from manufacturing

ISSUE	HAMILTON	JEFFERSON
Buying back bonds	1. ______________	2. ______________
Faith in common people	little	3. ______________
Promoting economic growth	4. ______________	should come from agriculture
Creating a national bank	should create a national bank	5. ______________
Interpreting the Constitution	6. ______________	strict construction

Name ______________ Class ______________ Date ______________

CHAPTER 11

The Expanding Nation

FORM C

CHAPTER TEST

MATCHING *3 points each* Place the letters of the descriptions next to the appropriate terms.

_____ **1.** judicial review

_____ **2.** Louisiana Purchase

_____ **3.** impressment

_____ **4.** Battle of Horseshoe Bend

_____ **5.** Napoleon Bonaparte

_____ **6.** Tecumseh

_____ **7.** Zebulon Pike

_____ **8.** Battle of New Orleans

_____ **9.** embargo

_____ **10.** Sacagawea

a. battle in which U.S. forces defeated the Creek Indians

b. Shoshone Indian woman who worked as a guide for Lewis and Clark

c. French leader who dreamed of rebuilding France's empire in North America

d. Shawnee leader who tried to unite American Indians from many regions

e. the practice of forcing people to serve in an army or navy

f. power of the Supreme Court to declare an act of Congress to be unconstitutional

g. battle in which U.S. forces, led by Andrew Jackson, badly defeated the British

h. young army officer sent to find the starting point of the Red River

i. region of land stretching from the Mississippi River to the Rocky Mountains that the United States bought from France

j. banning of trade

FILL IN THE BLANK *3 points each* Choose from the following list to complete each of the statements below.

Toussaint-Louverture	Harrison	Republican
Treaty of Ghent	Creek	Missouri
Supreme Court	American Indian	Embargo Act
War Hawks	Washington	Tripoli

1. At the same time that Thomas Jefferson won the presidency, the ______________ Party won control of both houses of Congress.

2. The justices who decided the *Marbury* v. *Madison* case agreed that the ______________ could not force the federal government to give Marbury his commission.

3. Former slave ______________ gained control of the French colony of Saint Domingue (present-day Haiti).

4. President Jefferson wanted Lewis and Clark to explore the ____________________ River region and establish peaceful relations with American Indians they met.

5. The United States sent the U.S. Navy to end pirate raids by the ____________________.

6. Congress passed the ____________________ in response to Britain's violations of U.S. neutrality.

7. Britain began giving military aid to ____________________ nations in the Northwest Territory in an effort to stop the rapid expansion of U.S. settlers into the region.

8. Tecumseh's American Indian confederacy fought William Henry ____________________ in the Battle of Tippecanoe.

9. Members of Congress who wanted to declare war against Britain were called ____________________.

10. General Andrew Jackson and his forces badly defeated the ____________________ Indians in the Battle of Horseshoe Bend.

11. The British burned the U.S. city of ____________________ during the War of 1812.

12. The ____________________ ended the War of 1812.

TRUE/FALSE *2 points each* Mark each statement *T* if it is true and *F* if it is false.

_____ **1.** *Marbury* v. *Madison* established the principle of judicial review.

_____ **2.** The United States bought the Louisiana Territory from Spain.

_____ **3.** Lewis and Clark began their expedition near St. Louis.

_____ **4.** Zebulon Pike led an expedition that traveled as far west as the Mississippi River.

_____ **5.** The Embargo Act was repealed because it did more harm to U.S. merchants than it did to Britain and France.

_____ **6.** Tecumseh led a confederation of southwestern Indians against the United States.

_____ **7.** Captain Oliver Hazard Perry led the U.S. Navy to victory in the Battle of Lake Erie after he flew a flag that said, "Don't give up the ship!"

_____ **8.** The U.S. victory in the Battle of New Orleans caused the British to finally agree to a peace treaty with the United States.

IDENTIFICATION *2 points each* Examine the map and complete the description of Lewis and Clark's expedition using the words listed below.

Lewis and Clark, 1804–1806

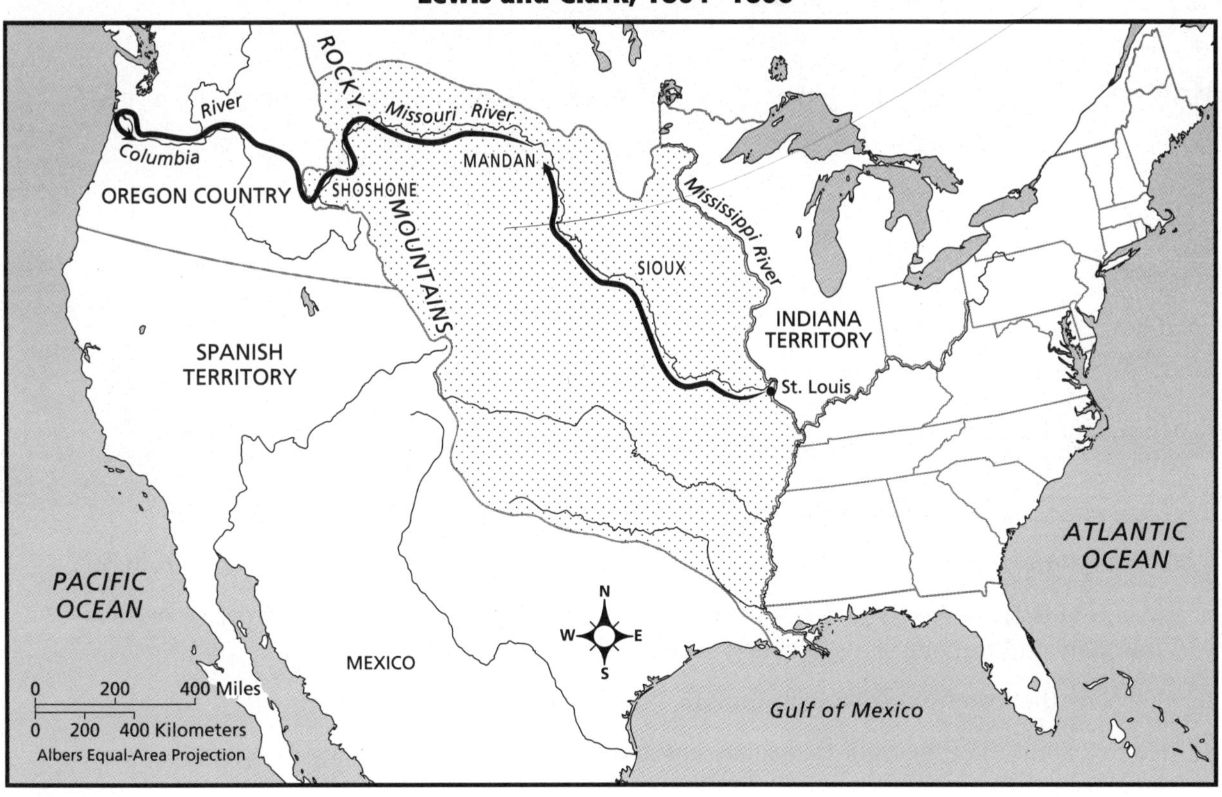

Shoshone	Oregon	Columbia
Mandan	Missouri	Sioux
Washington	Pacific	St. Louis

They went from near (1) ______________________ up the (2) ______________________ River, and traveled through the lands of the (3) ______________________ and (4) ______________________ Indians. After Lewis and Clark crossed the Plains, they were helped across the Rocky Mountains by the (5) ______________________ Indians. They then followed the (6) ______________________ River, which lies between the present-day states of (7) ______________________ and (8) ______________________, and finally reached the (9) ______________________ Ocean.

CHAPTER 12

Name ______________________ Class ____________ Date ____________

A New National Identity — FORM C

CHAPTER TEST

MATCHING *3 points each* Place the letters of the descriptions next to the appropriate terms.

_____ **1.** Monroe Doctrine

_____ **2.** Trail of Tears

_____ **3.** Missouri Compromise

_____ **4.** nullification

_____ **5.** Whig Party

_____ **6.** Indian Removal Act

_____ **7.** Hudson River School

_____ **8.** Democratic Party

_____ **9.** Erie Canal

_____ **10.** spoils system

a. act that authorized the removal of American Indians who lived east of the Mississippi River

b. group of artists who celebrated the beauty of the American landscape in their work

c. statement that declared that North and South America were off-limits to future colonization

d. agreement that allowed Missouri to enter the Union as a slave state and Maine to enter as a free state and forbade slavery in new territories or states north of 36° 30´

e. waterway that ran from Albany to Buffalo, New York

f. idea that states had the right to disobey any federal law with which they disagreed

g. political party that backed Andrew Jackson

h. 800-mile forced march of Cherokee people to Indian Territory from 1838 to 1839

i. practice of rewarding supporters with government jobs

j. political party that supported the idea of a weak president and a strong legislature

FILL IN THE BLANK *3 points each* Choose from the following list to complete each of the statements below.

Seminole	Cumberland Road	nominating conventions
Adams-Onís	James Fenimore Cooper	Indian Territory
American System	*Worcester* v. *Georgia*	Rush-Bagot
Panic of 1837	Choctaw	Catharine Maria Sedgwick

1. Meetings that are organized to select a political party's presidential and vice presidential candidates are called ______________________ .

2. The first federal road project was the ______________________ .

3. Starting in the 1830s, the U.S. government began moving American Indians in the Southeast to an area called ______________________ .

4. In 1819 Spain gave all of Florida to the United States in the ______________________ Treaty.

5. In 1832 the Supreme Court declared that the federal government, not the state of Georgia, had authority over the Cherokee Nation in the ruling ____________________ .

6. The plan for using high tariffs to pay for internal improvements became known as the ____________________ .

7. Shortly after Martin Van Buren became president, the country experienced a financial crisis called the ____________________ .

8. Britain and the United States agreed to limit naval power on the Great Lakes in the ____________________ Agreement.

9. The author of *Last of the Mohicans* was ____________________ .

10. The ____________________ Indians gave up more than 10 million acres of their land to the state of Mississippi in the Treaty of Dancing Rabbit Creek.

11. The U.S. Army had to finally give up fighting the ____________________ , who fought to remain on their land in Florida for many years.

12. The author who rejected the idea that all women should get married was named ____________________ .

TRUE/FALSE *2 points each* Mark each statement *T* if it is true and *F* if it is false.

_____ **1.** When voting rights were changed in the 1820s and 1830s, more women and African Americans gained the right to vote.

_____ **2.** Simón Bolívar led many of the independence movements in Latin America.

_____ **3.** In the Convention of 1818, the United States gained fishing rights off the coasts of Labrador and Newfoundland, Canada, and established a border between the United States and Canada.

_____ **4.** John Quincy Adams was a popular and well-supported president.

_____ **5.** The state of Georgia removed the Cherokee to Indian Territory because the tribe had made no efforts to adopt the practices of white society.

_____ **6.** In 1832 the South Carolina state legislature passed a resolution declaring that it would not support the tariffs of 1828 and 1832 passed by the U.S. Congress.

_____ **7.** A controvery arose when Missouri applied to enter the Union as a slave state because this would upset the balance of slave and free states.

_____ **8.** Andrew Jackson was viewed by most Americans as a member of the upper class who distanced himself from the common people.

IDENTIFICATION *3 points each* Complete the following chart about Indian removal using the information below.

- Florida
- Cherokee
- they protected runaway slaves
- gold was discovered on their land
- Illinois
- Choctaw

AMERICAN INDIAN NATION	STATE OF RESIDENCE	REASON FOR REMOVAL
Sauk	1. ______________	to make room for white settlers
2. ______________	Mississippi	to make room for white settlers
3. ______________	Georgia	4. ______________
Seminole	5. ______________	6. ______________

UNIT 5

Name ______________ Class __________ Date __________

Building a Strong Nation

FORM C

UNIT TEST

MATCHING *3 points each* Place the letters of the descriptions next to the appropriate terms.

_____ **1.** judicial review

_____ **2.** Louisiana Purchase

_____ **3.** Trail of Tears

_____ **4.** Missouri Compromise

_____ **5.** nullification

_____ **6.** Tecumseh

_____ **7.** spoils system

_____ **8.** Battle of New Orleans

_____ **9.** Monroe Doctrine

_____ **10.** Sacagawea

a. statement that declared that North and South America were off-limits to future colonization

b. region stretching from the Mississippi River to the Rocky Mountains, which the United States bought from France

c. the practice of rewarding supporters with government jobs

d. Shawnee leader who tried to unite American Indians from many regions

e. agreement that allowed Missouri to enter the Union as a slave state and Maine to enter as a free state and forbid slavery in new territories or states north of 36° 31´

f. power of the Supreme Court to declare an act of Congress to be unconstitutional

g. battle in which U.S. forces, led by Andrew Jackson, badly defeated the British

h. 800-mile forced march of Cherokee people to Indian Territory from 1838 to 1839

i. Shoshone woman who worked as a guide for Lewis and Clark

j. idea that states had the right to disobey any federal law with which they disagreed

FILL IN THE BLANK *3 points each* Choose from the following list to complete each of the statements below.

Toussaint-Louverture	Cumberland Road	Panic of 1837
Rush-Bagot	Choctaw	Missouri
Supreme Court	Treaty of Ghent	Seminole
Creek	War Hawks	American System

1. The ____________________ gave up more than 10 million acres of their land to the state of Mississippi in the Treaty of Dancing Rabbit Creek.

2. The justices who decided the *Marbury* v. *Madison* case agreed that the ____________________ could not force the federal government to give Marbury his commission.

3. Former slave ____________________ gained control of the French colony Saint Domingue (present-day Haiti).

4. President Jefferson wanted Lewis and Clark to explore the ____________________ River region and establish peaceful relations with American Indians they met.

5. The first federal road project was the ____________________ .

6. Shortly after Martin Van Buren became president, the country experienced a financial crisis called the ____________________ .

7. Britain and the United States agreed to limit naval power on the Great Lakes in the ____________________ Agreement.

8. The plan for using high tariffs to pay for internal improvements became known as the ____________________ .

9. Members of Congress who wanted to declare war against Britain were called ____________________ .

10. General Andrew Jackson and his forces badly defeated the ____________________ Indians in the Battle of Horseshoe Bend.

11. The U.S. Army had to finally give up fighting the ____________________ , who fought to remain on their land in Florida for many years.

12. The ____________________ ended the War of 1812.

TRUE/FALSE *2 points each* Mark each statement *T* if it is true and *F* if it is false.

_____ **1.** When voting rights were changed in the 1820s and 1830s, more women and African Americans gained the right to vote.

_____ **2.** The United States bought the Louisiana Territory from France.

_____ **3.** Andrew Jackson was viewed by most Americans as an upper-class man who distanced himself from the common people.

_____ **4.** Zebulon Pike led an expedition that traveled as far west as the Mississippi River.

_____ **5.** The Embargo Act was repealed because it did more harm to U.S. merchants than it did to Britain and France.

_____ **6.** The state of Georgia removed the Cherokee to Indian Territory because the tribe had made no efforts to adopt the practices of white society.

_____ **7.** Simón Bolívar led many of the independence movements in Latin America.

_____ **8.** U.S. victory in the Battle of New Orleans caused the British to finally agree to a peace treaty with the United States.

IDENTIFICATION *3 points each* Complete the following chart about Indian removal using the information below.

- Florida
- Cherokee
- they protected runaway slaves
- gold discovered on their land
- Illinois
- Choctaw

AMERICAN INDIAN NATION	STATE OF RESIDENCE	REASON FOR REMOVAL
Sauk	1. ____________	to make room for white settlers
2. ____________	Mississippi	to make room for white settlers
3. ____________	Georgia	4. ____________
Seminole	5. ____________	6. ____________

CHAPTER 13

Name ______________________ Class ____________ Date ____________

Industrial Growth in the North — FORM C

★ ★ ★ ★ ★ ★ ★ ★ ★ ★ ★ ★ ★ ★ ★ ★ ★ ★ ★ ★

CHAPTER TEST

MATCHING *3 points each* Place the letters of the descriptions next to the appropriate terms.

_____ **1.** technology

_____ **2.** mass production

_____ **3.** textiles

_____ **4.** trade unions

_____ **5.** strike

_____ **6.** Industrial Revolution

_____ **7.** Rhode Island system

_____ **8.** telegraph

a. production of large numbers of identical goods

b. groups created by workers to improve pay and working conditions for workers

c. device that sends electrical signals through a wire to send messages across great distances

d. period of fast growth in use of machines for making goods

e. practice of hiring families to work in textile mills

f. cloth items

g. refusal to work until employers meet workers' demands

h. tools that are used to produce goods or to do work

FILL IN THE BLANK *2 points each* Choose from the following list to complete each of the statements below.

Lowell girls	Lowell system	*Tom Thumb*
railroad	Transportation Revolution	steamboat
steam power	*Clermont*	interchangeable parts
workday	sewing machines	Morse code

1. The ____________________ was a period of fast growth in the speed and ease of moving from one place to another.

2. Eli Whitney came up with the idea of using ____________________ to build and repair guns quickly and easily.

3. The young women who worked at the Lowell mills became known as ____________________.

4. Union supporters fought hard for better working conditions and for a 10-hour ____________________.

5. The combination of hiring young women and putting both spinning and weaving machines in one mill became known as the ____________________.

6. Robert Fulton's steamboat was called the ____________________ .

7. Peter Cooper raced his steam-powered locomotive, the ____________________, against a railcar pulled by horses.

8. At times, ____________________ travel could be dangerous because the coal engines could explode.

9. Each letter of the alphabet is represented by a series of long and short pulses in ____________________ .

10. The telegraph grew side by side with the ____________________ .

11. More and more factory owners changed from water power to ____________________ .

12. Many women bought ____________________ to try to earn a living out of their homes by making clothing.

TRUE/FALSE *2 points each* Mark each statement *T* if it is true or *F* if it is false.

_____ 1. At the beginning of the 1700s, the job of making clothing usually fell to female family members.

_____ 2. Most of the early mills in the United States were built in the South.

_____ 3. Many mill owners found it difficult to get people to work in factories.

_____ 4. Most factory workers worked for 12–14 hours a day.

_____ 5. Most factory owners wanted their workers to join unions.

_____ 6. Sarah Bagley became the second woman to be elected president of a labor union.

_____ 7. The fastest transportation many people had ever experienced during the mid-1800s was the train, which averaged around 20 miles per hour.

_____ 8. Morse's telegraph machine did not work the first time he tried to show it to the public.

IDENTIFICATION *3 points each* Complete the graphic organizer by selecting the name of a person from the following list and matching it to the correct description.

Elias Howe
Richard Arkwright
Samuel Morse
Francis Cabot Lowell
Martin Van Buren
Samuel Slater
John Deere
Robert Fulton
Isaac Singer
Cyrus McCormick
Eli Whitney
Sarah Bagley

NAME	DESCRIPTION
1. ______________________	British mechanic who came to the United States and taught Americans how to build spinning machines and factories
2. ______________________	inventor who came up with the idea of interchangeable parts to make and repair guns quickly and easily
3. ______________________	factory owner who came up with the ideas of hiring young women and having both spinning and weaving machines in his mills
4. ______________________	vice president of the New England Workingmen's Association who fought for a 10-hour workday
5. ______________________	U.S. president who gave many federal workers 10-hour workdays
6. ______________________	inventor of the first useable steamship
7. ______________________	invented the water frame to speed the production of cotton thread
8. ______________________	inventor of the telegraph and the creator of the code used to send messages by it
9. ______________________	inventor of the steel plow
10. ______________________	inventor of the mechanical reaper
11. ______________________	factory apprentice who invented the sewing machine
12. ______________________	improved upon and made a fortune from selling sewing machines

Name ______________________ Class ______________ Date ______________

CHAPTER 14

Agricultural Changes in the South FORM C

CHAPTER TEST

MATCHING *2 points each* Place the letters of the desciptions next to the appropriate terms.

_____ **1.** cotton gin

_____ **2.** cotton belt

_____ **3.** factors

_____ **4.** scientific agriculture

_____ **5.** yeomen

_____ **6.** trickster

_____ **7.** drivers

a. crop brokers who managed the trade between planters and their customers

b. men who made sure that slaves followed orders and who carried out punishments

c. the use of scientific methods to improve crop production

d. owners of small farms

e. machine that separated cotton fiber from the seeds

f. region that grew most of the cotton in the United States; from South Carolina to east Texas

g. clever character in folktales used to show slaves how to survive by outsmarting slaveholders

FILL IN THE BLANK *3 points each* Choose from the following list to complete each of the statements below.

spirituals	liberty	planters
property	Tredegar Iron Works	slaves
demand	folktales	kidnap
Louisiana	*Southern Review*	Nat Turner's Rebellion

1. Many people believed that a nation founded on the ideal of ____________________ should not enslave people.

2. U.S. farmers had trouble keeping up when the growing textile industry raised the ____________________ for cotton.

3. The state of ____________________ was the nation's leader in the sugar industry.

4. Joseph R. Anderson owned the ____________________, one of the most productive iron works in the nation.

5. Hugh Swinton Legaré published many of the works of the writers of the Charleston School in the ____________________ .

6. Large-scale farmers called ____________________ owned more than 20 slaves.

7. To keep a sense of community, ______________________ placed great importance on family and religion.

8. Some slaves sang emotional songs called ______________________ to express their religious beliefs.

9. Stories called ______________________ contained lessons about how to survive under slavery.

10. The most violent slave rebellion in the United States was ______________________ .

11. Most slaveholders and slave traders viewed slaves only as ______________________ .

12. Some dishonest slave traders would ______________________ free African Americans from the North and sell them into slavery.

TRUE/FALSE *2 points each* Mark each statement *T* if it is true or *F* if it is false.

_____ **1.** The development of cotton as a cash crop raised the demand for slaves.

_____ **2.** By 1860 cotton made up more than half of all U.S. exports.

_____ **3.** The South's main foreign trade partner was Great Britain.

_____ **4.** The major port city of the central United States was Houston.

_____ **5.** Most white southerners did not own slaves.

_____ **6.** Most yeoman families lived in comfort and let their slaves do the hard work.

_____ **7.** Very poor whites survived by stealing from planters.

_____ **8.** There were no slaves in southern cities.

_____ **9.** Most slaves who ran away did so for short periods of time, often to see relatives, and they usually returned on their own.

_____ **10.** Some slaves were allowed to earn money from odd jobs during their own time.

IDENTIFICATION *5 points each* Place the following crops on the map in the place or places in which they were mostly grown. Color in large areas such as the cotton belt with a colored pencil.

- cotton
- corn
- wheat
- sugarcane
- tobacco
- hemp and flax

Southern States

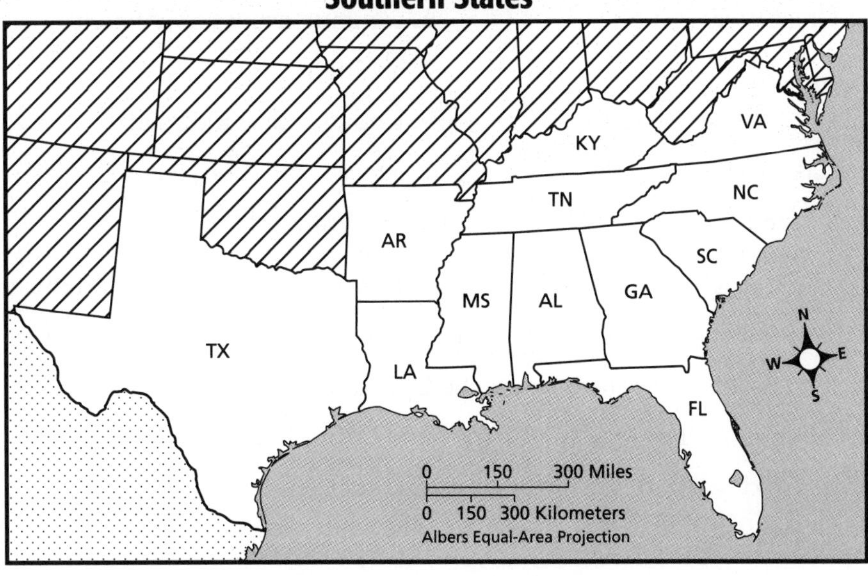

CHAPTER 15

Name ______________________ Class ______________ Date ______________

New Movements in America

FORM C

CHAPTER TEST

MATCHING *3 points each* Place the letters of the descriptions next to the appropriate terms.

______ **1.** Second Great Awakening

______ **2.** utopian community

______ **3.** nativists

______ **4.** middle class

______ **5.** temperance movement

______ **6.** common-school movement

______ **7.** abolition

______ **8.** Underground Railroad

______ **9.** Seneca Falls Convention

______ **10.** Declaration of Sentiments

a. gathering of women's rights activists that launched the organized women's rights movement

b. reform effort that tried to get people to give up or limit their drinking of alcohol

c. revival of Christian beliefs that spread across the United States during the 1790s and early 1800s

d. effort to have children of all classes and backgrounds educated together

e. group of people working together to create a perfect society

f. complete end to slavery

g. network of antislavery activists who helped escaped slaves

h. document that described beliefs about social injustice towards women

i. Americans who opposed immigration because they felt that immigrants presented a cultural and economic threat

j. social and economic level between the wealthy and the poor

FILL IN THE BLANK *3 points each* Choose from the following list to complete each of the statements below.

Harriet Tubman	transcendentalism	Sojourner Truth
Thomas Gallaudet	women's rights movement	crime
romantic movement	Lucretia Mott	Dorothea Dix
Frederick Douglass	epidemics	Susan B. Anthony

1. The idea that people could rise above material things is called ______________________ .

2. Poets and writers in the ______________________ explored ideas about spiritual renewal, simplicity, and nature.

3. Unsanitary conditions in cities often led to ______________________ .

4. Cities became centers of ______________________ because there was not enough police protection.

5. Because she supported herself financially, ____________________ was particularly interested in improving women's economic status.

6. Along with Elizabeth Cady Stanton, ____________________ organized the Seneca Falls Convention in 1848.

7. After studying in France for two years, ____________________ opened the first free U.S. school for people with hearing impairments.

8. As a result of the efforts of ____________________ and other reformers, many states created special hospitals for the mentally ill.

9. The most famous conductor on the Underground Railroad was ____________________ .

10. One of the best-known abolitionist speakers was ____________________ , who described the hardships he had experienced as a slave.

11. Many women who had been involved in the abolition movement also became involved in the ____________________ .

12. As a former slave, ____________________ spoke aggressively on both abolition and women's rights.

TRUE/FALSE *2 points each* Mark each statement *T* if it is true or *F* if it is false.

_____ **1.** Charles Grandison Finney went against traditional Protestant beliefs by preaching that each person was responsible for his or her own salvation.

_____ **2.** The Second Great Awakening attracted more men than women.

_____ **3.** The romantic movement was based on the idea that one's view of the world is best expressed through reason and logic rather than emotion.

_____ **4.** All abolitionists fought to free enslaved African Americans and to give them rights equal to other Americans.

_____ **5.** Supporters of the colonization movement felt that if free African Americans went to Africa to start new colonies it would prevent conflicts between the races in the United States.

_____ **6.** All white southerners were against abolition.

_____ **7.** Women's rights had been an important national issue since colonial times.

_____ **8.** One of the greatest accomplishments of the women's rights movement of the mid-1800s was that more women than ever began getting involved in women's rights issues.

IDENTIFICATION *3 points each* Complete the graphic organizer by filling in the problem that matches each solution or reform effort listed below.

- Alcohol abuse was causing problems in society.
- Free African Americans received an irregular education, or no education at all.
- Visually impaired and hearing-impaired Americans had trouble getting an education.
- Uneducated people were unable to better themselves.
- The mentally ill were placed in prison with criminals.
- Women had trouble getting an education beyond grade school.

PROBLEM	SOLUTION/REFORM EFFORT
1. ______________________________	States created special hospitals for the mentally ill.
2. ______________________________	Many states outlawed the selling of alcohol.
3. ______________________________	The common-school movement tried to establish a public school system to educate all children.
4. ______________________________	Reformers worked to start colleges for women and to convince existing colleges to accept women.
5. ______________________________	Some white schools began accepting African Americans, and colleges for African Americans were established.
6. ______________________________	People began learning how to meet the needs of visually impaired and hearing-impaired people and established special schools for them.

UNIT 6

Name ______________ Class ______________ Date ______________

A Changing Nation

FORM C

★ ★ ★ ★ ★ ★ ★ ★ ★ ★ ★ ★ ★ ★ ★ ★ ★ ★ ★ ★

UNIT TEST

MATCHING *3 points each* Place the letters of the descriptions next to the appropriate terms.

_____ **1.** cotton belt

_____ **2.** mass production

_____ **3.** Underground Railroad

_____ **4.** cotton gin

_____ **5.** Rhode Island system

_____ **6.** Industrial Revolution

_____ **7.** Second Great Awakening

_____ **8.** telegraph

a. production of large numbers of identical goods

b. revival of Christian beliefs that spread across the United States during the 1790s and early 1800s

c. device that sends electrical signals through a wire to send messages across great distances

d. fast growth in use of machines for making goods

e. practice of hiring families to work in textile mills

f. region that grew most of the cotton in the United States; from Georgia to east Texas

g. network of antislavery activists who helped fugitives escape slavery

h. machine that separated cotton fiber from the seeds

FILL IN THE BLANK *3 points each* Choose from the following list to complete each of the statements below.

property	Transportation Revolution	*Clermont*
spirituals	Lucretia Mott	Nat Turner's Rebellion
Dorothea Dix	Lowell system	transcendentalism
Frederick Douglass	planters	interchangeable parts

1. The ____________________ was a fast growth in the speed and ease of moving from one place to another.

2. Eli Whitney came up with the idea of using ____________________ to build and repair guns quickly and easily.

3. Large-scale farmers called ____________________ owned more than 20 slaves.

4. The idea that people could rise above the pursuit of wealth and material things is called ____________________ .

5. The combination of hiring young women and putting both spinning and weaving machines in one mill became known as the ____________________ .

6. The most violent slave rebellion in the United States was ____________________ .

7. As a result of the efforts of ____________________ and other reformers, many states created special hospitals for the mentally ill.

8. Some slaves sang emotional songs called ____________________ to express their religious beliefs.

9. Robert Fulton's steamboat was called the ____________________ .

10. One of the best-known abolitionist speakers was ____________________ , who described the hardships he had experienced as a slave.

11. Along with Elizabeth Cady Stanton, ____________________ organized the Seneca Falls Convention in 1848.

12. Most slaveholders and slave traders viewed slaves only as ____________________ .

TRUE/FALSE *2 points each* Mark each statement *T* if it is true or *F* if it is false.

_____ **1.** All abolitionists fought to free enslaved African Americans and to give them rights equal to other Americans.

_____ **2.** Most white southerners did not own slaves.

_____ **3.** Many mill owners found it difficult to get people to work in factories.

_____ **4.** The romantic movement was based on the idea that one's view of the world is best expressed through reason and logic rather than emotion.

_____ **5.** Most factory owners wanted their workers to join unions.

_____ **6.** There were no slaves in southern cities.

_____ **7.** The fastest transportation many people had ever experienced during the mid-1800s was the train, which averaged about 20 miles per hour.

_____ **8.** By 1860 cotton made up more than half of all U.S. exports.

IDENTIFICATION *4 points each* Complete the graphic organizer by filling in the problem that matches each solution or reform effort listed below.

- Alcohol abuse was causing problems in society.
- Free African Americans received an irregular education, or no education at all.
- Visually impaired and hearing-impaired Americans had trouble getting an education.
- Uneducated people were unable to better themselves.
- The mentally ill were placed in prison with criminals.
- Women had trouble getting an education beyond grade school.

PROBLEM	SOLUTION/REFORM EFFORT
1. ______________________	States created special hospitals for the mentally ill.
2. ______________________	Many states outlawed the selling of alcohol.
3. ______________________	The common-school movement tried to establish a public school system to educate all children.
4. ______________________	Reformers worked to get colleges for women and to convince existing colleges to accept women.
5. ______________________	Some white schools began accepting African Americans, and colleges for African Americans were established.
6. ______________________	People began learning how to meet the needs of visually impaired and hearing-impaired people and established special schools for them.

CHAPTER 16

Name ______________________ Class ______________ Date ______________

Expanding West

FORM C

CHAPTER TEST

MATCHING *3 points each* Place the letters of the descriptions next to the appropriate terms.

_____ **1.** Californios

_____ **2.** mountain men

_____ **3.** Donner Party

_____ **4.** Alamo

_____ **5.** annex

_____ **6.** Tejanos

_____ **7.** Battle of San Jacinto

_____ **8.** *empresarios*

_____ **9.** Sutter's Fort

_____ **10.** rendezvous

a. group of pioneers stranded in the Sierra Nevada along the California Trail, many of whom died

b. agents contracted by Mexico to bring settlers to Texas

c. fur trappers and traders who traveled to the Rocky Mountains and Pacific Northwest

d. colony in California established by a Swiss immigrant

e. last battle of the Texas Revolution

f. Spanish colonists in Texas

g. to take control of

h. an old mission that Texas rebels occupied

i. Spanish colonists in California

j. once a year gathering of mountain men, who met to trade and socialize

FILL IN THE BLANK *3 points each* Choose from the following list to complete each of the statements below.

Father Miguel Hidalgo y Costilla	missionaries	Oregon Trail
New Mexico	California Trail	Republic of Texas
George Catlin	American Indians	Stephen F. Austin
Germany	Sutter's Fort	slaves

1. The oldest and most important province on New Spain's northern frontier was ______________________ .

2. The leader of one of the first groups of Americans to settle in Texas was ______________________ .

3. The first leader of a rebellion against Spanish rule in Mexico was ______________________ .

4. Many American settlers ignored Mexican laws by bringing ______________________ into Texas.

5. The independent nation of Texas was called the ____________________ .

6. Under Mirabeau Lamar, ____________________ were forced to leave their homelands in Texas.

7. The largest group of European immigrants to Texas was from ____________________ .

8. Many of the settlers moving to Oregon Country traveled there on the ____________________ .

9. Marcus and Narcissa Whitman were ____________________ who settled in Walla Walla in present-day Washington State, and established a mission called Waiilatpu.

10. The southern branch of the Oregon Trail was called the ____________________ .

11. Established by a Swiss immigrant, ____________________ , became a popular resting place for settlers going to California.

12. A famous artist who moved West to paint scenes of American Indians was ____________________ .

TRUE/FALSE *2 points each* Mark each statement *T* if it is true and *F* if it is false.

_____ **1.** The leader who finally declared Mexico an independent nation was army officer Agustín de Iturbide.

_____ **2.** After Mexico won its independence, wealthy Californios were able to establish huge *empresarios*.

_____ **3.** Texans won the battle at the Alamo, which led to the independence of Texas.

_____ **4.** The commander in chief of the Texas army during the Texas war for independence was Sam Houston.

_____ **5.** The Republic of Texas encouraged immigration from the United States and Europe by offering land grants to settlers.

_____ **6.** Many mountain men bought land and established farms high in the mountains of the West.

_____ **7.** The Cayuse Indians adopted Marcus and Narcissa Whitman into their tribe, and helped spread Christianity to other American Indians in Oregon Country.

_____ **8.** In the mid-1800s, most people living in California were still American Indians and Mexicans.

IDENTIFICATION *3 points each* Complete the following graphic organizer about the Texas war for independence by filling in the blanks with items listed below.

- win
- loss
- James Fannin
- Alamo
- Goliad
- Sam Houston and Juan Seguín

BATTLE	LEADER(S) OF TEXAS FORCES	WIN OR LOSS FOR TEXANS
1. ______________	William Travis and Jim Bowie	2. ______________
3. ______________	4. ______________	loss
San Jacinto	5. ______________ and ______________	6. ______________

CHAPTER 17

Name ______________________ Class ____________ Date ____________

Manifest Destiny and War

FORM C

CHAPTER TEST

MATCHING *3 points each* Place the letters of the descriptions next to the appropriate terms.

_____ **1.** Mormons

_____ **2.** manifest destiny

_____ **3.** Treaty of Guadalupe Hidalgo

_____ **4.** Mormon Trail

_____ **5.** prospect

_____ **6.** Mexican Cession

_____ **7.** Bear Flag Revolt

_____ **8.** Gadsden Purchase

_____ **9.** forty-niners

a. to search for gold

b. people who came to California in 1849 to search for gold

c. 1846 uprising in California to make the area an independent republic

d. document that marked the end of the Mexican War

e. idea that U.S. growth from the Atlantic Ocean to the Pacific Ocean was unstoppable and unavoidable

f. payment for land that included the southern parts of what are now Arizona and New Mexico

g. Mexican territory turned over to the United States after the Mexican War

h. people who followed the teachings of Joseph Smith

i. westward route to Utah

FILL IN THE BLANK *3 points each* Choose from the following list to complete each of the statements below.

John Sutter	John Tyler	John O'Sullivan
James K. Polk	Winfield Scott	Zachary Taylor
Henry David Thoreau	Henry Clay	John C. Frémont
Brigham Young	James Marshall	Biddy Mason

1. General ____________________, known as "Old Fuss and Feathers," captured Mexico City in 1847.

2. President ____________________ wanted to expand the South's power by annexing Texas.

3. After the 1844 presidential election, ____________________ claimed that his victory was based on support for annexation

4. Captain ____________________ fought in the Bear Flag Revolt.

5. Mormons followed ____________________ to Utah.

6. Writer ____________________ went to jail because he would not pay taxes that might support a war.

7. The California Gold Rush began after ____________________ discovered gold in 1848.

8. During his presidential campaign, ____________________ initially opposed the annexation of Texas.

9. Newspaper editor ____________________ believed that the annexation of Texas was unavoidable.

10. Former slave ____________________ became one of California's richest landowners.

11. General ____________________ led troops into southern Texas to support U.S. claims to the region.

12. Workers at ____________________'s mill quit to search for gold.

TRUE/FALSE *2 points each* Mark each statement *T* if it is true or *F* if it is false.

_____ **1.** Supporters of expansion hoped that people would move from eastern cities to the frontier.

_____ **2.** Ralph Waldo Emerson believed that the Mexican War would unite Americans.

_____ **3.** All forty-niners traveled to California by sea.

_____ **4.** Chinese immigrants were not generally welcomed by Americans.

_____ **5.** The United States and Great Britain disagreed over the border between the United States and Canada.

_____ **6.** Individual miners generally dug mines deep beneath the earth's surface.

_____ **7.** Mormons did not think discipline was important in a community.

_____ **8.** Land laws caused conflict between Mexican Americans living in the southwest and the U.S. government.

_____ **9.** Mining camps were well-organized and had little unrest.

_____ **10.** Mexican soldiers defeated U.S. troops at Veracruz in 1847.

_____ **11.** The main Mormon settlement in the West was Salt Lake City.

IDENTIFICATION *5 points each* Examine the drawing below and answer the questions that follow.

1. What is the man in the picture doing?

____

____

2. What kind of equipment is he using?

____

____

3. Where might this equipment have been used?

____

____

Name ____________________ Class ____________ Date ____________

The Nation Expands West

FORM C

UNIT TEST

MATCHING *3 points each* Place the letters of the descriptions next to the appropriate terms.

_____ **1.** Californios

_____ **2.** Mormons

_____ **3.** Mexican Cession

_____ **4.** Alamo

_____ **5.** Gadsden Purchase

_____ **6.** Tejanos

_____ **7.** Battle of San Jacinto

_____ **8.** *empresarios*

_____ **9.** forty-niners

_____ **10.** Treaty of Guadalupe Hidalgo

a. people who came to California in 1849 to search for gold

b. people who followed the teachings of Joseph Smith

c. document that marked the end of the Mexican War

d. land turned over to the United States after the Mexican War

e. last battle of the Texas independence movement, which was won by the Texans

f. Spanish colonists in Texas

g. agents contracted by Mexico to bring settlers to Texas

h. old Franciscan mission that Texas rebels occupied

i. Spanish colonists in California

j. payment for land that included the southern part of what are now Arizona and New Mexico

FILL IN THE BLANK *3 points each* Choose from the following list to complete each of the statements below.

Father Miguel Hidalgo y Costilla	John C. Frémont	Oregon Trail
New Mexico	California Trail	Republic of Texas
James Marshall	Winfield Scott	Zachary Taylor
Brigham Young	Sutter's Fort	John O'Sullivan

1. The oldest and most important province on New Spain's northern frontier was ____________________.

2. General ____________________, known as "Old Fuss and Feathers," captured Mexico City in 1847.

3. The first leader of a rebellion against Spanish rule in Mexico was ____________________.

4. Mormons followed ____________________ to Utah.

5. The independent nation of Texas was called the ____________________ .

6. The gold rush began after ____________________ discovered gold in 1847.

7. Newspaper editor ____________________ believed that the annexation of Texas was unavoidable.

8. Many of the settlers moving to Oregon Country traveled there on the ____________________ .

9. Captain ____________________ fought in the Bear Flag Revolt.

10. The southern branch of the Oregon Trail was called the ____________________ .

11. Established by a Swiss immigrant, ____________________ , became a popular resting place for settlers going to California.

12. General ____________________ led troops into southern Texas to support U.S. claims to the region.

TRUE/FALSE *2 points each* Mark each statement *T* if it is true or *F* if it is false.

_____ **1.** The leader who finally declared Mexico an independent nation was army officer Agustín de Iturbide.

_____ **2.** Supporters of expansion hoped that people would move from eastern cities to the frontier.

_____ **3.** Chinese immigrants were generally welcomed by Americans.

_____ **4.** The commander in chief of the Texas army during the Texas war for independence was Mirabeau Lamar.

_____ **5.** The Republic of Texas encouraged immigration from the United States and Europe by offering land grants to settlers.

_____ **6.** Many mountain men bought land and established farms high in the mountains of the West.

_____ **7.** Land laws caused conflict between Mexican American settlers and the U.S. government.

_____ **8.** Mining camps were well-organized and had little unrest.

IDENTIFICATION *6 points each* Examine the drawing below and answer the questions that follow.

1. What is the man in the picture doing?

____

____

2. What kind of equipment is he using?

____

____

3. Where might this equipment have been used?

____

____

Name ______________ Class ______________ Date ______________

CHAPTER 18

A Divided Nation

FORM C

CHAPTER TEST

MATCHING *3 points each* Place the letter of the correct definition next to each term.

_____ **1.** popular sovereignty

_____ **2.** sectionalism

_____ **3.** Fugitive Slave Act

_____ **4.** Crittenden Compromise

_____ **5.** Constitutional Union Party

_____ **6.** Free-Soil Party

_____ **7.** Republican Party

_____ **8.** Freeport Doctrine

_____ **9.** Pottawatomie Massacre

_____ **10.** secession

a. political party formed by antislavery northerners before the presidential election of 1848

b. act of formally withdrawing from the Union

c. the killing of five pro-slavery men in Kansas by John Brown and a group of followers

d. political party formed in 1860 that supported the U.S. Constitution, the Union, and the enforcement of the laws

e. made it a federal crime to assist runaway slaves and allowed fugitive slaves to be arrested even in areas where slavery was illegal

f. proclamation by Stephen Douglas that only the people in a territory, not the Supreme Court, had the authority to decide whether slavery should be legal in that territory

g. devotion to the interests of one region instead of to the country as a whole

h. principle that would allow voters in a territory to decide whether they wanted to ban or permit slavery

i. plan introduced to Congress to prevent secession and avoid civil war

j. political party formed in 1854 to oppose the spread of slavery in the West

FILL IN THE BLANK *3 points each* Choose from the following list to complete each of the statements below.

Harriet Beecher Stowe	"Bleeding Kansas"	Compromise of 1850
John Brown	South Carolina	Democratic
Jefferson Davis	Frederick Douglass	Abraham Lincoln
Stephen Douglas	Dred Scott	Kansas-Nebraska Act

1. In her book *Uncle Tom's Cabin,* ______________ described the evils of slavery.

2. The ______________ brought California into the Union as a free state and divided the rest of the Mexican Cession into two territories.

3. An abolitionist named ______________ was hanged for leading a raid at Harpers Ferry, Virginia.

4. The law that divided the remainder of the Louisiana Purchase into two territories was called the

_____________________.

5. Lincoln was involved in a series of famous debates with _____________________.

6. One of the most famous slave narratives was written by the former slave

_____________________.

7. Although he sued for his freedom, _____________________ lost his case in the Supreme Court.

8. After the formation of the Confederate States of America, _____________________ was elected president of the Confederacy.

9. In 1860 _____________________ was elected president; soon after, several states seceded from the Union.

10. Because of the violence that erupted in this state, it was nicknamed _____________________.

11. Before the election of 1860, the _____________________ Party split into two groups over the issue of slavery.

12. The first state to secede from the Union was _____________________.

TRUE/FALSE *2 points each* Mark each statement *T* if it is true or *F* if it is false.

_____ **1.** Most Californians did not want slavery in their state.

_____ **2.** Most abolitionists opposed the Fugitive Slave Act.

_____ **3.** In the Compromise of 1850 California entered as a slave state and Maine as a free state.

_____ **4.** Franklin Pierce won the presidential election of 1852.

_____ **5.** The town of Lawrence, Kansas was attacked and burned by a large group of proslavery men.

_____ **6.** In the *Dred Scott* decision, the Supreme Court declared that African Americans were not citizens and that Scott's status depended on the laws of Missouri.

_____ **7.** In the Lincoln-Douglas debates, Lincoln argued that African Americans were equal to whites in all ways.

_____ **8.** The Confederate States of America based their constitution on the U.S. Constitution.

IDENTIFICATION *2 points each* Complete the graphic organizer by selecting the individual from the following list and matching them to the correct statement.

Stephen Douglas	Roger Taney	Martin Van Buren
Harriet Beecher Stowe	Abraham Lincoln	David Wilmot
Lewis Cass	Henry Clay	John Bell

1. ______________	wrote about the evils of slavery
2. ______________	debated with Lincoln and introduced the Kansas-Nebraska Act to find a compromise in planning a railroad to the Pacific
3. ______________	introduced a proposal to keep slavery out of the Mexican Cession
4. ______________	main author of the Compromise of 1850
5. ______________	Michigan senator who strongly supported the idea of popular sovereignty
6. ______________	Republican presidential candidate in 1860
7. ______________	candidate for the Free Soil Party in the presidential election of 1848
8. ______________	chief justice of the United States who ruled in the *Dred Scott* decision
9. ______________	ran as the Constitutional Union candidate in the 1860 presidential election

CHAPTER 19

Name ______________________ Class ______________ Date ______________

The Civil War

FORM C

CHAPTER TEST

MATCHING *3 points each* Place the letters of the descriptions next to the appropriate terms or names.

_____ **1.** Copperheads

_____ **2.** Emancipation Proclamation

_____ **3.** ironclads

_____ **4.** Battle of Gettysburg

_____ **5.** Ulysses S. Grant

_____ **6.** Vicksburg

_____ **7.** cotton diplomacy

_____ **8.** Fort Sumter

_____ **9.** Battle of Antietam

_____ **10.** Robert E. Lee

a. Confederate use of the cotton trade to try to convince Britain to support them in the war

b. Union general who led victories in the West and forced the final surrender of Confederate forces

c. attacked by Confederate forces signalling the start of the Civil War

d. Lincoln's order that freed slaves in areas rebelling against the Union

e. bloodiest single-day battle of the war

f. battle that marked the turning point of the war

g. Confederate general who surrendered to the Union at Appomattox Courthouse

h. city that suffered a six-week-long attack by the Union

i. northern Democrats who opposed the war

j. iron-plated ships used in war

FILL IN THE BLANK *3 points each* Choose from the following list to complete each of the statements below.

Gettysburg Address	First Battle of Bull Run	draft
Dorothea Dix	54th Massachusetts Infantry	border states
Battle of Pea Ridge	Dr. Elizabeth Blackwell	Andersonville
William Tecumseh Sherman	Appomattox Courthouse	total war

1. The slave states of Delaware, Kentucky, Missouri, and Maryland were called ______________________.

2. Both the North and the South used a ______________________ to recruit soldiers for their armies.

3. The first woman to receive a license to practice medicine, ______________________, pressured President Lincoln to form the U.S. Sanitary Commission to provide medical services to soldiers.

4. At the ______________________, Confederate troops forced Union soldiers to retreat and ruined Union hopes of winning the war quickly.

5. A group of American Indians fought on the side of the Confederacy in the ______________________.

6. A regiment of mainly free African Americans called the ______________________ played a central role in the capture of Fort Wagner in South Carolina.

7. More than 3,000 women served as paid nurses in the Union army under the leadership of ______________________.

8. The worst prison camp conditions were found at ______________________, in southwestern Georgia.

9. In the spring of 1864, General ______________________ led Union forces in the capture of Atlanta, Georgia.

10. Confederate leader General Lee surrendered to General Grant in a town called ______________________.

11. After the Battle of Gettysburg, President Lincoln gave a famous speech called the ______________________ to Union forces.

12. On his March to the Sea, General Sherman practiced ______________________, which is the targeting of civilian as well as military resources.

TRUE/FALSE *2 points each* Mark each statement *T* if it is true or *F* if it is false.

______ **1.** The Confederacy had a better network of railways to move troops and supplies than the Union had.

______ **2.** Confederate forces won the Seven Days Battles as well as the Second Battle of Bull Run.

______ **3.** Union forces broke through the Confederate blockade of important ports by using blockade runners.

______ **4.** Union forces gained an advantage in taking control of the Mississippi River valley after General Grant won the Battle of Shiloh.

______ **5.** Some abolitionists thought that Lincoln had gone too far in issuing the Emancipation Proclamation.

______ **6.** Contrabands were escaped slaves in South Carolina who Lincoln allowed to serve in Union forces in 1862.

_____ **7.** During the war, Lincoln suspended *habeas corpus*, which is the constitutional protection against unlawful imprisonment.

_____ **8.** Women were not very involved in helping with the war effort in the North or the South.

IDENTIFICATION *2 points each* Show whether each statement applied most to the North or the South by writing "Confederacy" or "Union" before each statement.

1. ______________________	had a better network of railways to move troops and supplies
2. ______________________	had a long military tradition and a large number of talented officers
3. ______________________	had more shipyards to make naval vessels
4. ______________________	could more easily raise money to spend on the war effort
5. ______________________	wanted to blockade its enemy's seaports and strangle its economy
6. ______________________	wanted to control the Mississippi River, dividing the enemy and cutting its internal communications
7. ______________________	concentrated on winning foreign support, especially from Britain
8. ______________________	most factories located in the region held by this side
9. ______________________	did not need to conquer and occupy large amounts of enemy territory

UNIT 8

Name ______________________ Class ______________ Date ______________

The Nation Breaks Apart

FORM C

UNIT TEST

MATCHING *3 points each* Place the letters of the descriptions next to the appropriate terms or names.

_____ **1.** popular sovereignty

_____ **2.** Robert E. Lee

_____ **3.** Fugitive Slave Act

_____ **4.** sectionalism

_____ **5.** Ulysses S. Grant

_____ **6.** Battle of Gettysburg

_____ **7.** Pottawatomie Massacre

_____ **8.** Fort Sumter

_____ **9.** Emancipation Proclamation

_____ **10.** secession

a. Union general who led victories in the West and forced the final surrender of Confederate forces

b. act of formally withdrawing from the Union

c. killing of five pro-slavery men in Kansas by John Brown and a group of followers

d. battle that marked the turning point of the war

e. act that made it a federal crime to assist runaway slaves and allowed fugitive slaves to be arrested even in areas where slavery was illegal

f. Lincoln's order that freed all slaves in areas rebelling against the Union

g. devotion to the interests of one region instead of to the country as a whole

h. principle that would allow voters in a territory to decide whether they wanted to ban or permit slavery

i. attacked by Confederate forces signalling the start of the Civil War

j. Confederate general who surrendered at Appomattox Courthouse

FILL IN THE BLANK *3 points each* Choose from the following list to complete each of the statements below.

Harriet Beecher Stowe	John Brown	Gettysburg Address
First Battle of Bull Run	South Carolina	"Bleeding Kansas"
Dr. Elizabeth Blackwell	Andersonville	Abraham Lincoln
border states	Dred Scott	William Tecumseh Sherman

1. In her book *Uncle Tom's Cabin,* ____________________ focused on the evils of slavery.

2. The worst prison camp conditions were found at ____________________, in southwestern Georgia.

3. Because of the violence that erupted in this state, it was nicknamed ____________________.

4. An abolitionist named ____________________ was hanged for leading a raid at Harpers Ferry, Virginia.

5. The first woman to receive a license to practice medicine, ____________________, pressured President Lincoln to form the U.S. Sanitary Commission to provide medical services to soldiers.

6. In the spring of 1864, General ____________________ led Union forces in the capture of Atlanta, Georgia.

7. Although he sued for his freedom, ____________________ lost his case in the Supreme Court.

8. The slave states of Delaware, Kentucky, Missouri, and Maryland were called ____________________.

9. In 1860 ____________________ was elected president and soon after several states seceded from the Union.

10. After the Battle of Gettysburg President Lincoln gave a famous speech called the ____________________ to Union supporters.

11. At the ____________________, Confederate troops forced Union soldiers to retreat and ruined Union hopes of winning the war quickly.

12. The first state to secede from the Union was ____________________.

TRUE/FALSE *2 points each* Mark each statement *T* if it is true or *F* if it is false.

_____ 1. The Confederacy's network of railways to move troops and supplies was better than the Union's network.

_____ 2. The Confederate States of America based their constitution on the U.S. Constitution.

_____ 3. In the Compromise of 1850 California entered as a slave state and Maine as a free state.

_____ 4. During the war, Lincoln suspended *habeas corpus*, which is the constitutional protection against unlawful imprisonment.

_____ 5. The town of Lawrence, Kansas, was attacked and burned by a large group of pro-slavery men.

_____ 6. Women were not very involved in helping the war effort in the North or the South.

_____ 7. In the Lincoln-Douglas debates, Lincoln argued that African Americans were equal to whites in all ways.

_____ 8. Union forces gained an advantage in taking control of the Mississippi River valley after General Grant won the Battle of Shiloh.

IDENTIFICATION *2 points each* Show whether each statement applied most to the North or the South by writing "Confederacy" or "Union" before each statement.

1. ______________________	had a better network of railways to move troops and supplies
2. ______________________	had a long military tradition and a large number of talented officers
3. ______________________	had more shipyards to make naval vessels
4. ______________________	could more easily raise money to spend on the war effort
5. ______________________	wanted to blockade its enemy's seaports and strangle its economy
6. ______________________	wanted to control the Mississippi River, dividing the enemy and cutting its internal communications
7. ______________________	concentrated on winning foreign support, especially from Britain
8. ______________________	most factories located in the region held by this side
9. ______________________	did not need to conquer and occupy large amounts of enemy territory

CHAPTER 20

Name ______________________ Class ____________ Date ____________

Reconstruction **FORM C**

CHAPTER TEST

MATCHING *3 points each* Place the letters of the descriptions next to the appropriate terms.

_____ **1.** amnesty

_____ **2.** Jim Crow laws

_____ **3.** Civil Rights Act of 1866

_____ **4.** Reconstruction

_____ **5.** Redeemers

_____ **6.** Radical Republicans

_____ **7.** Freedmen's Bureau

_____ **8.** Ku Klux Klan

_____ **9.** sharecropping

_____ **10.** Black Codes

a. farming system in which land owners provided land, seeds, and tools in exchange for part of the crop

b. wanted the federal government to be very involved in reorganizing the South

c. southern Democrats who regained political power in the South after 1877 and who wanted to limit rights of African Americans

d. state laws that limited the freedom of African Americans

e. secret society that used violence to deny African Americans their rights

f. official government pardon

g. process of rebuilding the United States without slavery

h. laws that enforced segregation

i. organization started to help poor southerners

j. provided African Americans with the same legal rights as white Americans

FILL IN THE BLANK *3 points each* Choose from the following list to complete each of the statements below.

Reconstruction Acts	Fourteenth Amendment	segregation
Thirteenth Amendment	Panic of 1873	carpetbaggers
General Amnesty Act of 1872	*Plessy* v. *Ferguson*	Compromise of 1877
poll tax	scalawags	Fifteenth Amendment

1. The ______________________ helped cause financial problems that hurt the Republican party.

2. The ______________________ allowed many former Confederates to hold public office.

3. Slavery became illegal when the ______________________ was passed.

4. In ______________________ the Supreme Court established the idea of "separate-but-equal."

5. In the ____________________, Democrats agreed to accept Rutherford B. Hayes as president if all federal troops were removed from the South.

6. Northern Republicans who moved to the South were called ____________________.

7. The forced separation of African Americans and whites was called ____________________.

8. All African American men could vote after the ____________________ was passed.

9. Congress divided the South into military districts by passing the ____________________.

10. People had to pay a ____________________ before they could vote.

11. The ____________________ stated that all people born in the United States—except American Indians—were U.S. citizens.

12. Southern Republicans were called ____________________, which means mean fellows.

TRUE/FALSE *2 points each* Mark each statement *T* if it is true or *F* if it is false.

_____ 1. The most successful industry in the New South was fertilizer production.

_____ 2. President Abraham Lincoln thought that the South should be severely punished for breaking away from the Union.

_____ 3. After the Civil War, cotton prices dropped because too many farmers were planting that crop.

_____ 4. Members of the Ku Klux Klan attacked and sometimes murdered many African Americans.

_____ 5. Music was unpopular in the New South because many people were too unhappy to sing.

_____ 6. President Andrew Johnson was impeached because he tried to fire the Secretary of War.

_____ 7. Few African Americans voted for the Republican Party in the election of 1868.

_____ 8. Southern transportation and communications were destroyed during the Civil War.

_____ 9. Many former slaves chose new last names to show that they were free.

IDENTIFICATION *2 points each* Write the number of each item in the correct space to complete the graphic organizer and describe Reconstruction programs suggested by President Abraham Lincoln, the Wade-Davis Bill, and President Andrew Johnson.

1. offered pardon for all illegal acts during rebellion

2. states had to ban slavery

3. required oath of loyalty and ban on slavery

4. required presidential pardon for rich southerners and Confederate officers

5. permitted southerners to vote only if they swore they had never supported the Confederacy

6. gave amnesty to all southerners who took loyalty oath

7. returned all property except slaves

8. majority of adult males in state had to take loyalty oath

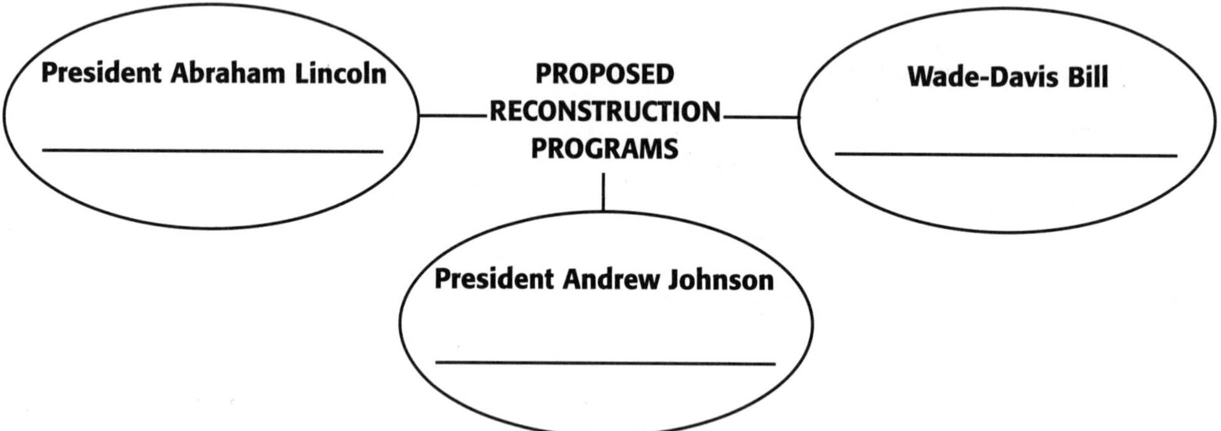

CHAPTER 21

Name ______________ Class ______________ Date ______________

The West

FORM C

CHAPTER TEST

MATCHING *4 points each* Place the letters of the descriptions next to the appropriate terms.

_____ **1.** bonanza

_____ **2.** Texas longhorn

_____ **3.** sodbusters

_____ **4.** reservations

_____ **5.** range wars

_____ **6.** boom towns

_____ **7.** Ghost Dance

_____ **8.** dry farming

_____ **9.** Dawes General Allotment Act

_____ **10.** Pony Express

a. conflicts between ranchers and farmers

b. nickname for Great Plains farmers

c. religious movement based on the idea of a paradise where Indians would live freely and the buffalo herds would return

d. shift to crops requiring less water

e. broke up reservation lands among individual Indians

f. sturdy, disease-resistant blend of Spanish and English cattle

g. group of horseback riders who carried mail along a 2,000-mile route

h. communities that grew suddenly when a mine opened

i. large deposit of precious ore

j. areas of federal land set aside for American Indians

FILL IN THE BLANK *2 points each* Choose from the following list to complete each of the statements below.

Comstock Lode	Pacific Railway Acts	Long Walk
range rights	transcontinental railroad	roundup
Fort Laramie Treaty	Homestead Act	Battle of the Little Bighorn
Massacre at Wounded Knee	Exodusters	Treaty of Medicine Lodge

1. During the ______________ the Navajo were forced to travel 300 miles across the desert to reach the reservation.

2. The ______________ accepted Indian claims to the Great Plains and allowed the United States to build forts and roads and to travel across the Plains.

3. A large silver and gold deposit in Nevada became known as the ______________ .

4. The Sioux defeated U.S. troops at the ______________ in 1876.

5. Most ranchers bought ____________________, or water rights, to control access to water during cattle drives.

6. African Americans who moved to Kansas became known as ____________________.

7. By signing the ____________________, many southern Plains Indians agreed to live on reservations.

8. The ____________________ gave railroad companies land in exchange for carrying U.S. mail and troops at lower rates.

9. The U.S. Army killed some 150 Sioux in the ____________________, the last major event of more than 25 years of war on the Great Plains.

10. The ____________________ provided land to farmers.

11. When the Union Pacific and the Central Pacific met in Promontory, Utah, the first ____________________ was complete.

12. During the ____________________, cattle were gathered to be transported to the market.

TRUE/FALSE *3 points each* Mark each statement *T* if it is true or *F* if it is false.

______ **1.** Working in a mine involved many physical dangers and health risks.

______ **2.** Cowboys borrowed the idea for tools such as the western saddle, the lariat, and leather chaps from Mexican ranch hands called vaqueros.

______ **3.** The Nez Percé escaped U.S. troops and settled in Canada.

______ **4.** Few people from other countries settled on the Great Plains.

______ **5.** In 1874 a swarm of grasshoppers destroyed many crops.

______ **6.** The Chisholm Trail ran from San Antonio, Texas, to Abilene, Kansas, and was a popular route for cattle drives.

______ **7.** Most workers on the Central Pacific railroad were Irish immigrants.

______ **8.** The Massacre at Wounded Knee marked the end of armed conflict between Indians and U.S. troops.

______ **9.** Railroads provided fast, inexpensive transportation and helped increase settlement in the West.

IDENTIFICATION *3 points each* Examine the drawing below and list three things this animal provided for the Plains Indians.

1. ______________________________

2. ______________________________

3. ______________________________

UNIT 9

Name ______________________ Class ______________ Date ______________

A Growing America FORM C

UNIT TEST

MATCHING *3 points each* Place the letters of the descriptions next to the appropriate terms.

_____ **1.** Radical Republicans

_____ **2.** sharecropping

_____ **3.** dry farming

_____ **4.** reservations

_____ **5.** Texas longhorn

_____ **6.** Jim Crow laws

_____ **7.** Ghost Dance

_____ **8.** Freedmen's Bureau

_____ **9.** Redeemers

_____ **10.** Pony Express

a. organization started to help poor southerners

b. southern Democrats who regained political power in the South after 1877 and who wanted to limit rights of African Americans

c. farming system in which land owners provided land, seeds, and tools in exchange for part of the crop

d. laws that enforced segregation

e. sturdy, disease-resistant blend of Spanish and English cattle

f. shift to crops requiring less water

g. group of horseback riders who carried mail along a 2,000-mile route

h. religious movement based on the idea of a paradise where American Indians would live freely and the buffalo herd would return

i. wanted the federal government to be very involved in reorganizing the South

j. government lands set aside for American Indians

FILL IN THE BLANK *3 points each* Choose from the following list to complete each of the statements below.

Homestead Act	Thirteenth Amendment	*Plessy* v. *Ferguson*
Fourteenth Amendment	transcontinental railroad	carpetbaggers
Compromise of 1877	Long Walk	Battle of the Little Bighorn
range rights	Fifteenth Amendment	Massacre at Wounded Knee

1. All African American men could vote after the ______________________ was passed.

2. The ______________________ provided land to farmers.

3. The ______________________ stated that all people born in the United States—except American Indians—were U.S. citizens.

4. Northern Republicans who moved to the South were called ______________________ .

5. During the ______________________ the Navajo were forced to travel 300 miles across the desert to reach the reservation.

6. Most ranchers bought ______________________, or water rights, to control access to water during cattle drives.

7. Slavery became illegal when the ______________________ was ratified.

8. In the ______________________, Democrats agreed to accept Rutherford B. Hayes as president if all federal troops were removed from the South.

9. The Sioux defeated U.S. troops at the ______________________ in 1876.

10. The U.S. Army killed some 150 Sioux in the ______________________, the last major event of more than 25 years of war on the Great Plains.

11. When the Union Pacific and the Central Pacific met at Promontory Point, the first ______________________ was complete.

12. In ______________________ the U.S. Supreme Court established the idea of "separate-but-equal."

TRUE/FALSE *2 points each* Mark each statement *T* if it is true or *F* if it is false.

_____ 1. After the Civil War, cotton prices dropped because too many farmers were planting that crop.

_____ 2. The most successful industry in the New South was fertilizer production.

_____ 3. Working in a mine involved many physical dangers and health risks.

_____ 4. The Massacre at Wounded Knee marked the end of armed conflict between American Indians and U.S. troops.

_____ 5. The Nez Percé escaped U.S. troops and settled in Canada.

_____ 6. President Andrew Johnson was impeached because he tried to fire the secretary of war.

_____ 7. Music was unpopular in the New South because many people were too unhappy to sing.

_____ 8. Few people from other countries settled on the Great Plains.

_____ 9. The Chisholm Trail ran from San Antonio, Texas, to Abilene, Kansas, and was a popular route for cattle drives.

IDENTIFICATION *2 points each* Write the number of each item in the correct space to complete the graphic organizer and describe Reconstruction programs suggested by President Abraham Lincoln, the Wade-Davis Bill, and President Andrew Johnson.

1. offered pardon for all illegal acts during rebellion

2. states had to ban slavery

3. required oath of loyalty and ban on slavery

4. required presidential pardon for rich southerners and Confederate officers

5. permitted southerners to vote only if they swore they had never supported the Confederacy

6. gave amnesty to all southerners who took loyalty oath

7. returned all property except slaves

8. majority of adult males in state had to take loyalty oath

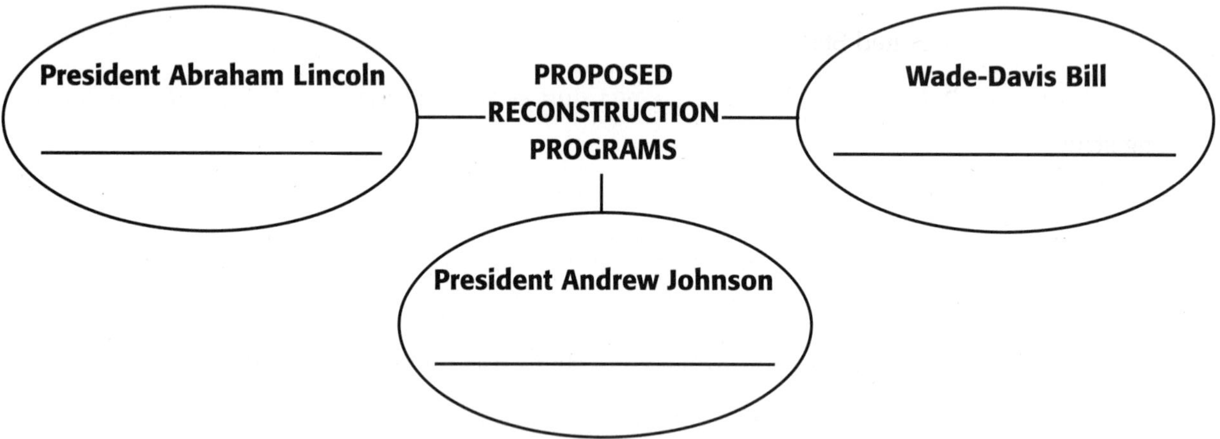

EPILOGUE

Name ______________________ Class ____________ Date ____________

Modern America **FORM C**

CHAPTER TEST

MATCHING *3 points each* Place the letters of the descriptions next to the appropriate terms.

_____ **1.** Sherman Antitrust Act

_____ **2.** Nineteenth Amendment

_____ **3.** Panama Canal

_____ **4.** Great Depression

_____ **5.** Cold War

_____ **6.** *Brown* v. *Board of Educaton*

_____ **7.** Equal Rights Amendment

_____ **8.** Tet Offensive

_____ **9.** Operation Desert Storm

_____ **10.** Contract with America

a. severe global economic decline that began with the crash of the U.S. stock market in October 1929

b. major attack that showed that the North Vietnamese were determined to keep fighting for South Vietnam

c. gave women in the United States the right to vote

d. decision by the U.S. Supreme Court that segregated public schools were unconstitutional

e. long struggle between the United States and the Soviet Union for world power

f. attempted to make monopolies and trusts that restrict free trade illegal

g. U.S.-led military effort to force Iraq's troops to leave Kuwait

h. built to connect the Atlantic and Pacific Oceans

i. plan supported by many Republicans that included a balanced budget and welfare reform

j. passed by Congress in 1972, but it was not ratified by the states

FILL IN THE BLANK *3 points each* Choose from the following list to complete each of the statements below.

Second Industrial Revolution	Freedom Rides	Iran-Contra affair
energy crisis	D-Day	progressives
Harlem Renaissance	federal deficit	United Nations
Eighteenth Amendment	Pullman Strike	Watergate

1. Civil rights activists participated in the ____________________ to challenge illegal segregation of bus stations in the South.

2. The ____________________ invasion of Nazi-occupied France broke through the German defenses, and Germany surrendered less than one year later.

3. The ____________________ was a period of enormous growth in U.S. manufacturing during the late 1800s.

4. The ____________________ were reformers who worked to solve the economic, social, and political problems caused by rapid city growth.

5. At the Yalta Conference, Churchill, Roosevelt, and Stalin agreed to create the ____________________ , an organization for settling international conflicts.

6. President Nixon resigned from office to avoid possible impeachment as a result of his participation in the ____________________ scandal.

7. The period of African American artistic accomplishment in the 1920s was called the ____________________ .

8. The Reagan administration spent hundreds of billions of dollars on a military buildup, contributing to a dramatic rise in the ____________________ .

9. When the Organization of Petroleum Exporting Countries raised the price of their oil, it led to an ____________________ in the United States.

10. The U.S. attorney general ended the ____________________ by ruling that it violated the Sherman Antitrust Act.

11. The ____________________ outlawed the manufacture, sale, and distribution of alcohol in the United States.

12. The ____________________ involved some top White House officials who illegally sold weapons and used the money to fund anticommunist rebels in Nicaragua.

TRUE/FALSE *2 points each* Mark each statement *T* if it is true or *F* if it is false.

______ **1.** The Civil Rights Act of 1964 banned all racial discrimination in the United States.

______ **2.** McCarthy claimed there were Communists in the U.S. government, but had little evidence.

______ **3.** The Seventeenth Amendment allowed state legislatures to elect U.S. senators.

______ **4.** The Treaty of Versailles ended World War I.

______ **5.** Many migrant workers left California because of the Dust Bowl to look for jobs in the Great Plains.

______ **6.** Under a system of free enterprise, businesses are run by the government.

______ **7.** The Truman Doctrine was President Truman's plan for winning the Korean War.

______ **8.** The New Deal was President Hoover's plan to deal with the Great Depression.

______ **9.** The Ku Klux Klan grew dramatically in the 1920s and targeted African Americans, Catholics, immigrants, Jews, and other groups.

_____**10.** The North American Free Trade Agreement allowed goods, people, and services to move freely among Canada, Mexico, and the United States.

_____**11.** The Gulf of Tonkin Resolution stopped President Johnson from sending additional troops to Vietnam.

_____**12.** In President Clinton's second term in office, the U.S. economy was strong and the federal government had a budget surplus.

IDENTIFICATION *2 points each* Complete the graphic organizer by writing the name of each U.S. president next to the appropriate policy.

- John Kennedy
- Lyndon Johnson
- Richard Nixon
- Gerald Ford
- Jimmy Carter

POLICY	PRESIDENT
détente with the Soviet Union	1. ______________________
Great Society	2. ______________________
Camp David Accords	3. ______________________
Bay of Pigs invasion	4. ______________________
pardon for Nixon	5. ______________________

ANSWER KEY

Chapter 1

FORM C

Matching

1. e
2. f
3. g
4. h
5. a
6. c
7. i
8. b
9. j
10. d

Fill in the Blank

1. migration
2. Mississippian
3. Aztec
4. totems
5. Jerusalem
6. monasteries
7. matrilineal
8. Mali
9. Muslims
10. Magna Carta
11. Silk Road
12. Kublai Khan

True/False

1. T
2. F
3. F
4. F
5. T
6. T
7. F
8. T

Identification

(names in order from chart)

Aztec
Leif Eriksson
Iroquois
Vikings
Paleo-Indians
William of Normandy
Maya
Pope Urban II
Mansa Musa
Zheng He

Chapter 2

FORM C

Matching

1. h
2. d
3. g
4. c
5. e
6. a
7. b
8. f
9. i

Fill in the Blank

1. Line of Demarcation
2. Renaissance
3. convert
4. circumnavigate
5. viceroy
6. Black Death
7. Treaty of Tordesillas
8. capital
9. caravel
10. *Reconquista*
11. joint-stock company
12. Northwest Passage

True/False

1. F
2. T
3. F
4. F
5. T
6. T
7. F
8. T
9. F
10. T
11. F

Identification

From Europe to the Americas	From the Americas to Europe
smallpox	corn
horses	cocoa
measles	potatoes
cattle	tobacco
typhus	

Unit 1

FORM C

Matching

1. k
2. h
3. d
4. f
5. a
6. j
7. c
8. b
9. e
10. g
11. i

Fill in the Blank

1. Renaissance
2. Mississippian
3. Aztec
4. circumnavigate
5. Jerusalem
6. monasteries
7. Black Death
8. *Reconquista*
9. Muslims
10. Magna Carta
11. Silk Road
12. Northwest Passage

True/False

1. T
2. T
3. F
4. F
5. T
6. F
7. T
8. F

Identification

From Europe to the Americas	From the Americas to Europe
smallpox	corn
horses	cocoa
measles	potatoes
cattle	tobacco
typhus	

Chapter 3

FORM C

Matching

1. f
2. b
3. c
4. d
5. j
6. h
7. a
8. e
9. i
10. g

Fill in the Blank

1. New Netherland
2. *encomienda* system
3. plantation
4. Protestants
5. borderlands
6. Inca
7. sea dogs
8. Aztec
9. England
10. Malintzin
11. New Amsterdam
12. Bartolomé de Las Casas

True/False

1. F
2. F
3. T
4. F
5. T
6. F
7. F
8. T
9. T

Identification

1. Juan de Oñate
2. Francisco Vásquez de Coronado
3. Juan Ponce de Leon
4. René-Robert de La Salle
5. Álvar Núñez Cabeza de Vaca
6. Louis Jolliet and Jacques Marquette
7. Juan Rodríguez Cabrillo
8. Hernando de Soto

Chapter 4

FORM C

Matching

1. e
2. i
3. g
4. f
5. a
6. h
7. c
8. j
9. d
10. b

Fill in the Blank

1. joint-stock company
2. Powhatan Confederacy
3. House of Burgesses
4. the Bible
5. Mayflower Compact
6. Thanksgiving
7. Massachusetts Bay Company
8. Salem witch trials
9. Catholics
10. Toleration Act of 1649
11. New York
12. Pennsylvania

True/False

1. T
2. F
3. F
4. T
5. T
6. F
7. F
8. T
9. F
10. F

Identification

1. g
2. h
3. a
4. e
5. d
6. b
7. f
8. c

Chapter 5

Form C

Matching

1. d
2. a
3. i
4. h
5. b
6. f
7. c
8. j
9. g
10. e

Fill in the Blank

1. assemblies
2. trade
3. imports
4. Middle Passage
5. cash crops
6. exports
7. apprentices
8. Privy Council
9. Scientific Revolution
10. staple crops
11. *New England Primer*
12. bicameral legislature

True/False

1. T
2. F
3. T
4. T
5. F
6. T
7. F
8. T

Identification

1. Benjamin Banneker
2. Anne Bradstreet
3. John Smibert
4. David Rittenhouse
5. Galileo Galilei
6. Benjamin Franklin
7. Phillis Wheatley
8. Sir Isaac Newton
9. John Locke
10. Jonathan Edwards

Unit 2

FORM C

Matching

1. f
2. b
3. c
4. j
5. a
6. h
7. i
8. d
9. e
10. g

Fill in the Blank

1. Middle Passage
2. *encomienda* system
3. House of Burgesses
4. Protestants
5. Mayflower Compact
6. *New England Primer*
7. sea dogs
8. Aztec
9. Powhatan Confederacy
10. bicameral legislature
11. New Amsterdam
12. Catholics

True/False

1. T
2. F
3. T
4. T
5. T
6. F
7. F
8. F
9. F

Identification

1. Juan de Oñate
2. Francisco Vásquez de Coronado
3. Juan Ponce de Leon
4. René-Robert de La Salle
5. Álvar Núñez Cabeza de Vaca
6. Louis Jolliet and Jacques Marquette
7. Juan Rodríguez Cabrillo
8. Hernando de Soto

Chapter 6

FORM C

Matching

1. d
2. h
3. i
4. c
5. a
6. b
7. e
8. f
9. j
10. g

Fill in the Blank

1. Fort Duquesne
2. George Grenville
3. Metacomet
4. Albany Plan of Union
5. Edward Braddock
6. Committees of Correspondence
7. Boston Massacre
8. Stamp Act
9. James Wolfe
10. James Otis
11. Boston Tea Party
12. Pontiac's Rebellion

True/False

1. T
2. F
3. T
4. F
5. T
6. T
7. F
8. T
9. F
10. T

Identification

1. The sign asks people to stop buying British products.
2. anyone who might have protested British taxation policies

Chapter 7

FORM C

Matching

1. h
2. i
3. a
4. f
5. d
6. e
7. c
8. g
9. b
10. j

Fill in the Blank

1. Deborah Sampson
2. George Washington
3. Thomas Paine
4. John Paul Jones
5. Salem Poor
6. Marquis de Lafayette
7. Francis Marion
8. Friedrich von Steuben
9. Thomas Jefferson
10. Thayendanegea
11. Comte de Rochambeau
12. William Howe

True/False

1. F
2. T
3. F
4. T
5. F
6. F
7. T
8. T
9. T
10. F
11. T
12. T
13. F
14. F

Identification

1. a, d, f
2. b, c, e

Unit 3

FORM C

Matching

1. b
2. d
3. i
4. e
5. h
6. a
7. c
8. f
9. j
10. g

Fill in the Blank

1. Thomas Paine
2. George Grenville
3. Friedrich von Steuben
4. Albany Plan of Union
5. Thomas Jefferson
6. George Washington
7. Boston Massacre
8. Stamp Act
9. James Wolfe
10. Marquis de Lafayette
11. Boston Tea Party
12. Comte de Rochambeau

True/False

1. F
2. F
3. T
4. F
5. T
6. T
7. T
8. T
9. T
10. F

Identification

1. 1, 4, 6
2. 2, 3, 5

Chapter 8

FORM C

Matching

1. d
2. g
3. f
4. i
5. h
6. c
7. a
8. e
9. b

Fill in the Blank

1. interstate commerce
2. suffrage
3. Constitutional Convention
4. *Federalist Papers*
5. Three-Fifths Compromise
6. Federalists
7. depression
8. Northwest Territory
9. federalism
10. bill of rights
11. Antifederalists
12. checks and balances

True/False

1. F
2. T
3. T
4. F
5. F
6. T
7. F
8. F
9. T
10. F
11. T

Identification

1. g
2. a, d
3. e
4. f
5. h
6. b, c, i

Chapter 9

FORM C

Matching

1. d
2. f
3. a
4. h
5. j
6. g
7. i
8. b
9. c
10. e

Fill in the Blank

1. apportionment
2. search warrant
3. deport
4. representative democracy
5. due process
6. political action committees
7. six
8. cabinet
9. First
10. jury
11. citizen
12. pardons

True/False

1. F
2. T
3. F
4. F
5. T
6. F
7. T
8. T

Identification

1. declaring war
2. running the postal system
3. conducting elections
4. regulating education
5. taxing
6. enforcing laws

Chapter 10

FORM C

Matching

1. d
2. a
3. c
4. b
5. e
6. f
7. i
8. h
9. g
10. j

Fill in the Blank

1. Twelfth Amendment
2. Judiciary Act
3. Edmond Genet
4. Farewell Address
5. political parties
6. bonds
7. precedent
8. U.S. Army
9. XYZ affair
10. Whiskey Rebellion
11. speculators
12. Bank of the United States

True/False

1. F
2. T
3. F
4. F
5. T
6. F
7. T
8. F

Identification

1. federal government should pay full price
2. paying full price cheats original owners
3. majority should rule
4. should come from manufacturing
5. should not create a national bank
6. loose construction

Unit 4

FORM C

Matching

1. f
2. c
3. g
4. i
5. j
6. e
7. a
8. d
9. b
10. h

Fill in the Blank

1. search warrant
2. Citizen Genet
3. Constitutional Convention
4. *Federalist Papers*
5. Three-Fifths Compromise
6. representative democracy
7. Bank of the United States
8. cabinet
9. Whiskey Rebellion
10. bill of rights
11. XYZ affair
12. apportionment

True/False

1. T
2. T
3. T
4. F
5. T
6. F
7. F
8. F
9. T
10. F
11. T

Identification

1. federal government should pay full price
2. paying full price cheats original owners
3. majority should rule
4. should come from manufacturing
5. should not create a national bank
6. loose construction

Chapter 11

FORM C

Matching

1. f
2. i
3. e
4. a
5. c
6. d
7. h
8. g
9. j
10. b

Fill in the Blank

1. Republican
2. Supreme Court
3. Toussaint-Louverture
4. Missouri
5. Barbary States
6. Embargo Act
7. American Indian
8. Harrison
9. War Hawks
10. Creek
11. Washington
12. Treaty of Ghent

True/False

1. T
2. F
3. T
4. F
5. T
6. F
7. T
8. F

Identification

1. St. Louis
2. Missouri
3. Sioux
4. Mandan
5. Shoshone
6. Columbia
7. Oregon
8. Washington
9. Pacific

Chapter 12

FORM C

Matching

1. c
2. h
3. d
4. f
5. j
6. a
7. b
8. g
9. e
10. i

Fill in the Blank

1. nominating conventions
2. Cumberland Road
3. Indian Territory
4. Adams-Onís
5. *Worcester* v. *Georgia*
6. American System
7. Panic of 1837
8. Rush-Bagot
9. James Fenimore Cooper
10. Choctaw
11. Seminole
12. Catharine Maria Sedgwick

True/False

1. F
2. T
3. T
4. F
5. F
6. T
7. T
8. F

Identification

1. Illinois
2. Choctaw
3. Cherokee
4. gold was discovered on their land
5. Florida
6. protected runaway slaves

Unit 5

FORM C

Matching

1. f
2. b
3. h
4. e
5. j
6. d
7. c
8. g
9. a
10. i

Fill in the Blank

1. Choctaw
2. Supreme Court
3. Toussaint-Louverture
4. Missouri
5. Cumberland Road
6. Panic of 1837
7. Rush-Bagot
8. American System
9. War Hawks
10. Creek
11. Seminole
12. Treaty of Ghent

True/False

1. F
2. T
3. F
4. F
5. T
6. F
7. T
8. F

Identification

1. Illinois
2. Choctaw
3. Cherokee
4. gold was discovered on their land
5. Florida
6. protected runaway slaves

Chapter 13

FORM C

Matching

1. h
2. a
3. f
4. b
5. g
6. d
7. e
8. c

Fill in the Blank

1. Transportation Revolution
2. interchangeable parts
3. Lowell girls
4. workday
5. Lowell system
6. *Clermont*
7. *Tom Thumb*
8. steamboat
9. Morse code
10. railroad
11. steam power
12. sewing machines

True/False

1. T
2. F
3. T
4. T
5. F
6. F
7. T
8. F

Identification

1. Samuel Slater
2. Eli Whitney
3. Francis Cabot Lowell
4. Sarah Bagley
5. Martin Van Buren
6. Robert Fulton
7. Richard Arkwright
8. Samuel Morse
9. John Deere
10. Cyrus McCormick
11. Elias Howe
12. Isaac Singer

Chapter 14

FORM C

Matching

1. e
2. f
3. a
4. c
5. d
6. g
7. b

Fill in the Blank

1. liberty
2. demand
3. Louisiana
4. Tredegar Iron Works
5. *Southern Review*
6. planters
7. slaves
8. spirituals
9. folktales
10. Nat Turner's Rebellion
11. property
12. kidnap

True/False

1. T
2. T
3. T
4. F
5. T
6. F
7. F
8. F
9. T
10. T

Identification

cotton: grown in most of the South from South Carolina to Texas

corn: Tennessee, Kentucky, Virginia

wheat: Maryland, Virginia

sugarcane: Louisiana

tobacco: North Carolina

hemp and flax: Tennessee and Kentucky

Chapter 15

FORM C

Matching

1. c
2. e
3. i
4. j
5. b
6. d
7. f
8. g
9. a
10. h

Fill in the Blank

1. transcendentalism
2. romantic movement
3. epidemics
4. crime
5. Susan B. Anthony
6. Lucretia Mott
7. Thomas Gallaudet
8. Dorothea Dix
9. Harriet Tubman
10. Frederick Douglass
11. women's rights movement
12. Sojourner Truth

True/False

1. T
2. F
3. F
4. F
5. T
6. F
7. F
8. T

Identification

1. The mentally ill were placed in prison with criminals.
2. Alcohol abuse was causing problems in society.
3. Uneducated people were unable to better themselves.
4. Women had trouble getting an education beyond grade school.
5. Free African Americans received an irregular education, or no education at all.
6. Visually impaired and hearing-impaired Americans had trouble getting an education.

Unit 6

FORM C

Matching

1. f
2. a
3. g
4. h
5. e
6. d
7. b
8. c

Fill in the Blank

1. Transportation Revolution
2. interchangeable parts
3. planters
4. transcendentalism
5. Lowell system
6. Nat Turner's Rebellion
7. Dorothea Dix
8. spirituals
9. *Clermont*
10. Frederick Douglass
11. Lucretia Mott
12. property

True/False

1. F
2. T
3. T
4. F
5. F
6. F
7. T
8. T

Identification

1. The mentally ill were placed in prison with criminals.
2. Alcohol abuse was causing problems in society.
3. Uneducated people were unable to better themselves.
4. Women had trouble getting an education beyond grade school.
5. Free African Americans received an irregular education, or no education at all.
6. Visually impaired and hearing-impaired Americans had trouble getting an education.

Chapter 16

FORM C

Matching

1. i
2. c
3. a
4. h
5. g
6. f
7. e
8. b
9. d
10. j

Fill in the Blank

1. New Mexico
2. Stephen F. Austin
3. Father Miguel Hidalgo y Costilla
4. slaves
5. Republic of Texas
6. American Indians
7. Germany
8. Oregon Trail
9. missionaries
10. California Trail
11. Sutter's Fort
12. George Catlin

True/False

1. T
2. F
3. F
4. T
5. T
6. F
7. F
8. T

Identification

1. Alamo
2. loss
3. Goliad
4. James Fannin
5. Sam Houston and Juan Seguín
6. win

Chapter 17

FORM C

Matching

1. h
2. e
3. d
4. i
5. a
6. g
7. c
8. f
9. b

Fill in the Blank

1. Winfield Scott
2. John Tyler
3. James K. Polk
4. John C. Frémont
5. Brigham Young
6. Henry David Thoreau
7. James Marshall
8. Henry Clay
9. John O'Sullivan
10. Biddy Mason
11. Zachary Taylor
12. Sutter's

True/False

1. T
2. F
3. F
4. T
5. T
6. F
7. F
8. T
9. F
10. F
11. T

Identification

1. panning for gold
2. a gold pan
3. a stream or river

Unit 7

FORM C

Matching

1. i
2. b
3. d
4. h
5. j
6. f
7. e
8. g
9. a
10. c

Fill in the Blank

1. New Mexico
2. Winfield Scott
3. Father Miguel Hidalgo y Costilla
4. Brigham Young
5. Republic of Texas
6. James Marshall
7. John O'Sullivan
8. Oregon Trail
9. John C. Frémont
10. California Trail
11. Sutter's Fort
12. Zachary Taylor

True/False

1. T
2. T
3. F
4. F
5. T
6. F
7. T
8. F

Identification

1. panning for gold
2. a gold pan
3. a stream or river

Chapter 18

FORM C

Matching

1. h
2. g
3. e
4. i
5. d
6. a
7. j
8. f
9. c
10. b

Fill in the Blank

1. Harriet Beecher Stowe
2. Compromise of 1850
3. John Brown
4. Kansas-Nebraska Act
5. Stephen Douglas
6. Frederick Douglass
7. Dred Scott
8. Jefferson Davis
9. Abraham Lincoln
10. "Bleeding Kansas"
11. Democratic
12. South Carolina

True/False

1. T
2. T
3. F
4. T
5. F
6. T
7. F
8. T

Identification

1. Harriet Beecher Stowe
2. Stephen Douglas
3. David Wilmot
4. Henry Clay
5. Lewis Cass
6. Abraham Lincoln
7. Martin Van Buren
8. Roger Taney
9. John Bell

Chapter 19

FORM C

Matching

1. i
2. d
3. j
4. f
5. b
6. h
7. a
8. c
9. e
10. g

Fill in the Blank

1. border states
2. draft
3. Dr. Elizabeth Blackwell
4. First Battle of Bull Run
5. Battle of Pea Ridge
6. 54th Massachusetts Infantry
7. Dorothea Dix
8. Andersonville
9. William Tecumseh Sherman
10. Appomattox Courthouse
11. Gettysburg Address
12. total war

True/False

1. F
2. T
3. F
4. T
5. T
6. T
7. T
8. F

Identification

1. Union
2. Confederacy
3. Union
4. Union
5. Union
6. Union
7. Confederacy
8. Union
9. Confederacy

Unit 8

FORM C

Matching

1. h
2. j
3. e
4. g
5. a
6. d
7. c
8. i
9. f
10. b

Fill in the Blank

1. Harriet Beecher Stowe
2. Andersonville
3. "Bleeding Kansas"
4. John Brown
5. Dr. Elizabeth Blackwell
6. William Tecumseh Sherman

7. Dred Scott
8. border states
9. Abraham Lincoln
10. Gettysburg Address
11. First Battle of Bull Run
12. South Carolina

True/False

1. F
2. T
3. F
4. T
5. T
6. F
7. F
8. T

Identification

1. Union
2. Confederacy
3. Union
4. Union
5. Union
6. Union
7. Confederacy
8. Union
9. Confederacy

Chapter 20

FORM C

Matching

1. f
2. h
3. j
4. g
5. c
6. b
7. i
8. e
9. a
10. d

Fill in the Blank

1. Panic of 1873
2. General Amnesty Act of 1872
3. Thirteenth Amendment
4. *Plessy* v. *Ferguson*
5. Compromise of 1877
6. carpetbaggers
7. segregation
8. Fifteenth Amendment
9. Reconstruction Acts
10. poll tax
11. Fourteenth Amendment
12. scalawags

True/False

1. F
2. F
3. T
4. T
5. F
6. T
7. F
8. T
9. T

Identification

President Abraham Lincoln—1, 3
President Andrew Johnson—4, 6, 7
Wade-Davis Bill—2, 5, 8

Chapter 21

FORM C

Matching

1. i
2. f
3. b
4. j
5. a
6. h
7. c
8. d
9. e
10. g

Fill in the Blank

1. Long Walk
2. Fort Laramie Treaty
3. Comstock Lode
4. Battle of the Little Bighorn
5. range rights
6. Exodusters
7. Treaty of Medicine Lodge
8. Pacific Railway Acts
9. Massacre at Wounded Knee
10. Homestead Act
11. transcontinental railroad
12. roundup

True/False

1. T
2. T
3. F
4. F
5. T
6. T
7. F
8. T
9. T

Identification

1. meat for food
2. hides for making clothing and tepees
3. horns for making cups and tools

Unit 9

FORM C

Matching

1. i
2. c
3. f
4. j
5. e
6. d
7. h
8. a
9. b
10. g

Fill in the Blank

1. Fifteenth Amendment
2. Homestead Act
3. Fourteenth Amendment
4. carpetbaggers
5. Long Walk
6. range rights
7. Thirteenth Amendment
8. Compromise of 1877
9. Battle of the Little Big Horn
10. Massacre at Wounded Knee
11. transcontinental railroad
12. *Plessy* v. *Ferguson*

True/False

1. T
2. F
3. T
4. T
5. F
6. T
7. F
8. F
9. T

Identification

1. President Abraham Lincoln—1, 3
2. President Andrew Johnson—4, 6, 7
3. Wade-Davis Bill—2, 5, 8

Epilogue

FORM C

Matching

1. f
2. c
3. h
4. a
5. e
6. d
7. j
8. b
9. g
10. i

Fill in the Blank

1. Freedom Rides
2. D-Day
3. Second Industrial Revolution
4. progressives
5. United Nations
6. Watergate
7. Harlem Renaissance
8. federal deficit
9. energy crisis
10. Pullman Strike
11. Eighteenth Amendment
12. Iran-Contra affair

True/False

1. F
2. T
3. F
4. T
5. F
6. F
7. F
8. F
9. T
10. T
11. F
12. T

Identification

1. Richard Nixon
2. Lyndon Johnson
3. Jimmy Carter
4. John Kennedy
5. Gerald Ford